The Best Summer Drinks

500 Incredible Cocktail and Appetizer Recipes

Ray Foley

SOURCEBOOKS, INC.
NAPERVILLE, ILLINOIS

Copyright © 2009 by Ray Foley
Cover and internal design © 2009 by Sourcebooks, Inc.
Cover design by Cyanotype Book Architects
Cover photo © iStockPhoto.com/Talshiar

Published by Sourcebooks, Inc.
P.O. Box 4410, Naperville, Illinois 60567-4410
(630) 961-3900
Fax: (630) 961-2168
www.sourcebooks.com

Library of Congress Cataloging-in-Publication Data

Foley, Ray.
  The best summer drinks : 500 incredible cocktail and appetizer recipes / by Ray Foley. -- 1st ed.
    p. cm.
  Includes index.
  1. Bartending. 2. Cocktails. I. Bartender magazine. II. Title.
  TX951.F592 2009
  641.8'74--dc22

                          2009008767

Printed and bound in the United States of America.
          CHG 10 9 8 7 6 5 4 3 2

Dedication

To all those who have supported me over the years, and especially Jaclyn Marie Foley.

The Best Summer Drinks

Contents

Acknowledgments

To all the brand managers, public relation firms, agencies, and suppliers who made *Bartender Magazine* successful and for all their input to *The Best Summer Drinks*.

I would also like to thank Peter Lynch, Sara Kase, and the people at Sourcebooks; Loretta Natiello; the Famous Foleys: Ray, William, and Amy; and also those on the other side of the bar tolerating me and, of course, the bartenders all over the world, who take the chance and serve me! And to Jaclyn Marie Foley, the love of my life, who makes my cup overflow and, of course, my main man Ryan. Also to Erin Mackey for her tremendous assistance in putting this book together.

Introduction

Summertime, and the living is easy. Time for fun, fresh cocktails, and light food. In *The Best Summer Drinks*, you'll find new cocktails with new products not to be found in any other book.

Some cocktails are cool and some frozen, but all will refresh your palate on a long summer's day. There is a cocktail for every sunny day, perfect for the beach, the lake, or the backyard. And for cloudy days, there are cocktails to chase your blues away.

So, pull up a lawn chair or beach chair after reading this refreshing book, and CHILL OUT with a cool cocktail!

For more cool summer cocktails, go to www.usbartender.com or www.bartender.com, or email barmag@aol.com.

Summer Cocktails

10 Cane Fizz

2 oz. 10 Cane rum
4 oz. San Pellegrino limonata or aranciata
Lemon, lime, or orange twist for garnish

Pour liquids into a highball glass over ice.
Garnish with a fruit twist.

10 Cane Flamingo

2 oz. 10 Cane rum
1¼ oz. pineapple juice
¼ oz. fresh-squeezed lime juice
¼ oz. grenadine

Shake vigorously with ice and strain into a
chilled cocktail glass.

10 Grand

1½ oz. 10 Cane rum
1 oz. Grand Marnier
2 oz. peach nectar
2 oz. pomegranate juice
1 oz. Moët et Chandon champagne
Pour the first four ingredients into a mixing glass. Add ice, and shake vigorously. Strain into a chilled martini glass, or serve on the rocks in a highball glass. Top with the champagne.

360 Apple Tree Hugger

1 oz. 360 vodka
1 oz. Sour Apple Pucker Schnapps
1 oz. sweet and sour mix (Dissolve 1 tsp. sugar in 3 oz. water. Add 2 oz. lemon juice.)

Shake with ice. Serve in a chilled glass or on the rocks.

360 Chocolate Conservation

1 oz. 360 vodka
½ oz. dark crème de cacao
½ oz. coffee liqueur
1 oz. half-and-half

Serve in a chilled glass or on the rocks.

360 Chocolate Sunset

1 oz. 360 vodka
½ oz. triple sec or premium orange liqueur
½ oz. dark crème de cacao
1 oz. half-and-half

Serve in a chilled glass or on the rocks.

360 Climate Cooler

1¼ oz. 360 vodka
¾ oz. triple sec
3 oz. fresh iced green tea
sugar or sweetener to taste

Shake with ice. Serve in a chilled glass or on the rocks. For added flavor, use your favorite flavored tea instead of the green tea.

360 Father Earth

1 oz. simple syrup (Dissolve 1 part sugar in 1 part boiling water. Let cool.)
2 oz. 360 vodka
2 strawberries, sliced
6 mint leaves, torn in half

Shake first two ingredients with ice. Strain, pour into a glass over the strawberries, and add the mint leaves.

360 Lemon Delight

1¼ oz. 360 vodka
¾ oz. triple sec
1 oz. sweet and sour mix (Dissolve 1 tsp. sugar
    in 3 oz. water. Add 2 oz. lemon juice.)
lemon wedge

Pour the first three ingredients into a shaker
over ice. Serve in a chilled glass or on the rocks.
Top with a squeeze of the lemon wedge.

360 Lights Out

1¼ oz. 360 vodka
¾ oz. raspberry liqueur
2 oz. sweet and sour mix (Dissolve 1 tsp. sugar
    in 3 oz. water. Add 2 oz. lemon juice.)
lemon slice for garnish

Shake liquids with ice. Serve in a chilled glass
or on the rocks. Garnish with the lemon slice.

360 Mellow Mango

1⅓ oz. 360 vodka
¾ oz. triple sec
1 ½ oz. mango purée or daiquiri mix
½ oz. orange juice
¾ oz. club soda or lemon-lime soda

Shake the first four ingredients with ice. Strain
into a glass over ice, and top with the soda.

360 Mother Earth

1¼ oz. 360 vodka
¾ oz. banana liqueur
2 oz. orange juice
1 oz. pineapple juice
¼ oz. grenadine

Shake first four ingredients with ice. Pour grenadine down the inside of the glass. Serve in a chilled glass or on the rocks.

360 New Leaf

4 lime wedges
6 mint leaves, torn in half
1 oz. simple syrup (Dissolve 1 part sugar in 1
    part boiling water. Let cool.)
2 oz. 360 vodka
1 oz. club soda or lemon-lime soda

Squeeze lime wedges, and drop into a glass. Muddle lime wedges, mint leaves, and simple syrup. Add the vodka, and top with soda. Shake with ice. Serve in a chilled glass or on the rocks.

360 Peach Tree Hugger

1 oz. 360 vodka
1 oz. peach schnapps
3 oz. cranberry juice
lemon slice for garnish

Shake first three ingredients and strain into in a chilled glass or serve on the rocks. Garnish with a lemon slice.

360 Planetary Punch

1¼ oz. 360 vodka
¾ oz. melon liqueur
½ oz. peach purée or daiquiri mix
1 oz. orange juice
1 oz. pineapple juice

Shake with ice. Serve in a chilled glass or on the rocks.

360 Solar Flare

1½ oz. 360 vodka
2 strawberries, sliced
6 mint leaves, torn in half
1 oz. simple syrup (Dissolve 1 part sugar in 1 part boiling water. Let cool.)
1–2 oz. lemon-lime soda

Muddle vodka, strawberries, mint leaves, and simple syrup in a glass. Add ice, and top with the lemon-lime soda.

360 Taboo

1¼ oz. 360 vodka
¾ oz. raspberry-flavored vodka
½ oz. chocolate syrup
1 oz. half-and-half

Serve in a chilled glass or on the rocks.

360 Ying Yang Chocolate

1¼ oz. 360 vodka
¾ oz. chocolate liqueur
½ oz. Irish Cream
1 oz. half-and-half
¼ oz. chocolate syrup

Shake with ice. Serve in a chilled glass or on the rocks.

Absolut Citron Colada

1½ oz. Absolut Citron vodka
1 oz. Marie Brizard Banana Liqueur
3 oz. pineapple juice
3 oz. piña colada mix
⅛ oz. lime juice
2 tbs. sugar
Pineapple slice for garnish
Coconut slice for garnish

Combine the first six ingredients in a blender; add 1 cup ice. Blend, and pour into a glass. Garnish with the pineapple and coconut slices.

Absolut Kurant Freeze

1½ oz. Absolut kurant vodka
1 oz. Marie Brizard banana liqueur
5 fresh raspberries
½ fresh banana
2 tbsp. sugar

Blend with 1 cup ice.

Acapulco Gold

1¼ oz. José Cuervo Especial tequila
⅝ oz. Grand Marnier
1 oz. sweet and sour mix (Dissolve 1 tsp. sugar
    in 3 oz. water. Add 2 oz. lemon juice.)

Blend with ice.

After-Glow

1 oz. DeKuyper melon liqueur
2 oz. vodka
1 oz. orange juice
Dash lemon juice

Shake with ice and strain into a glass over ice.
Serve very cold.

Alice-Be-Bananaless

¾ oz. vodka
¾ oz. amaretto
¾ oz. Midori melon liqueur
1 oz. cream

Build over ice in a shaker. Shake, and strain into a 7-oz. rocks glass over ice.

Ali-Colada

2 oz. Alizé red passion
Dash Bacardi rum
3 oz. piña colada mix
Pineapple wedge for garnish

Blend the first three ingredients with ice until smooth. Pour into a piña colada glass, and garnish with the pineapple wedge.

Alizé Dreamsicle

1½ oz. Alizé red passion
½ oz. Absolut vodka
2 oz. pineapple juice
2 oz. orange juice
½ oz. Coco Lopez cream of coconut
1 tbsp. Major Peters' grenadine

Blend with ice.

Alizé Mai Tai

2 oz. Alizé red passion
1 oz. white rum
2 oz. pineapple juice
2 oz. orange juice
1 oz. dark rum

Blend the first four ingredients. Pour into a glass, and float the dark rum on top.

Alizé Red Passion Lemonade

2 oz. Alizé red passion
3 oz. lemonade
Lemon twist for garnish

Shake and pour into a tall glass over ice. Garnish with the lemon twist.

Alizé Transfusion

2 oz. Alizé gold passion
1 oz. coconut-flavored rum
1½ oz. cranberry juice

Blend and serve in a rocks glass over ice.

All American Blue

2 oz. SKYY vodka
1 oz. blue curaçao
2 oz. white grape juice
Splash soda
1 slice lime or green apple for garnish

Shake the first three ingredients vigorously. Pour into a highball glass over ice. Top with the soda, and garnish with the fruit slice.

All That Razz

2 oz. Bacardi razz
1 oz. peach schnapps
Splash cranberry juice
Splash pineapple juice

Shake with ice and serve on the rocks.

Americano

1 oz. Campari
1 oz. Cinzano
Splash club soda
Orange twist for garnish

Pour the first two ingredients into a rocks highball glass over ice. Add a splash of club soda, and garnish with the orange twist.

Amethyst

5 lime wedges
¼ oz. agave nectar
1 oz. 1800 select silver tequila
¼ oz. VeeV açai liqueur
¼ oz. açai juice

Muddle the lime wedges with the agave nectar in the bottom of a shaker. Add remaining ingredients, shake vigorously, and pour into a rocks glass.

Apéritif

1 oz. 1800 select silver tequila
1 oz. Campari
1 oz. SOHO lychee liqueur
2 oz. grapefruit juice
1 slice blood orange, grapefruit, or orange
   for garnish

Pour the first four ingredients into a glass over ice, and garnish with the fruit slice.

Aphrodisiac

4–5 fresh strawberries plus 4 extra sliced for
    garnish
2 oz. Remy Martin VSOP
¼ oz. simple syrup (Dissolve 1 part sugar in 1
    part boiling water. Let cool.)
¼ oz. fresh pomegranate juice
1 oz. pressed apple juice

Muddle 4–5 strawberries. Strain juice into a
shaker over ice, and add liquids. Shake vigorously. Strain into a highball glass over ice, and
garnish with the sliced strawberries.

Apple Blossom Martini

1 oz. Marie Brizard Manzanita
¼ oz. Marie Brizard Madagascar vanilla
1 oz. Sobieski vodka

Pour ingredients into a shaker over ice. Strain
into a cocktail glass.

Bacardi Grasshopper

1 oz. Bacardi rum
¼ oz. green crème de menthe
½ oz. cream

Shake or blend with ice, and strain into a
cocktail glass.

Bacardi Roman Holiday

½ tsp. simple syrup (Dissolve 1 part sugar in
   1 part boiling water. Let cool.)
½ tsp. lemon juice
½ tsp. orange juice
½ cup unsweetened pineapple juice
½ oz. peach brandy
1 oz. Bacardi Superior rum
1 oz. Bacardi Gold rum
Club soda to top
Diced pineapple for garnish
1 strawberry, sliced, for garnish

Mix the first seven ingredients in a 14-oz.
glass. Stir in ice cubes and chilled club soda.
Float the diced pineapple and strawberry
slices on top as garnish.

Bacardi Rum Runner

¼ oz. Bacardi amber rum plus extra to top
⅞ oz. blackberry brandy
⅞ oz. banana liqueur
⅝ oz. grenadine
½ oz. lime juice

Blend with ice. Serve in an iced champagne
glass with a swirl of Bacardi Amber rum on top.

Bacardi Sombrero Cooler

3 oz. pineapple-grapefruit juice
2 oz. Bacardi rum
Orange slice for garnish

Mix liquids in an 8-oz. glass half filled with ice.
Garnish with the orange slice.

Bacardi Sparkler

1½ oz. Bacardi rum
¼ oz. dry vermouth
¼ oz. curaçao
¼ oz. lemon or lime juice
Maraschino cherry for garnish

Shake with ice and strain into a cocktail glass
or coconut shell. Garnish with the cherry.

Backdraft

1 oz. Drambuie
1 oz. Cointreau

Serve as a shot.

Bailey's Banana Colada

2 oz. Bailey's Irish cream
1 oz. Captain Morgan Parrot Bay coconut rum
1 banana

Blend with ice and pour into a glass.

Bailey's Coconut Frappé

2 oz. Bailey's Irish cream
1 oz. Malibu rum
2 oz. milk
Toasted coconut flakes for garnish

Shake or blend the first three ingredients until frothy. Pour over ice, and garnish with the toasted coconut flakes.

Bailey's Malibu Slide

1 oz. Bailey's Irish cream
1 oz. Kahlúa
1 oz. Malibu coconut rum

Blend with ice, and serve in a rocks or margarita glass.

Banana Banshee

1½ oz. crème de bananes
½ oz. white crème de cacao
1 scoop vanilla ice cream
Pineapple slice for garnish

Blend liquids until smooth. Pour into a tall glass, and garnish with the pineapple slice.

Banana Daiquiri

1½ oz. rum
½ oz. crème de bananes
½ ripe banana, sliced
Juice 1 lime

Blend until smooth. Pour, unstrained, into a tall chilled glass.

Banana Man

1 oz. Bacardi rum
¼ oz. lemon juice or Rose's lime juice
½ tsp. sugar
1 banana

Blend with ice until smooth. Pour into a tall glass.

Banana Mudslide

¼ oz. Kahlúa
¼ oz. Carolans Irish cream
½ oz. Hiram Walker crème de bananes
½ oz. Stolichnaya vodka
1 oz. milk or cream

Blend with ice until smooth. Pour into a tall glass.

Banilla Boat

1 oz. Drambuie
½ oz. DeKuyper crème de bananes
4 oz. vanilla ice cream
Splash Chambord
Banana slice for garnish
1 filbert for garnish

Blend the first three ingredients until smooth. Serve in a champagne glass, and top with the Chambord. Garnish with the banana slice and filbert.

Barbados Punch

1 oz. Tommy Bahama white sand rum
$\frac{1}{3}$ oz. premium orange liqueur
$1\frac{3}{4}$ oz. pineapple juice
Juice $\frac{1}{2}$ lime
$1\frac{3}{4}$ oz. orange juice
2 dashes grenadine
$\frac{2}{3}$ oz. Tommy Bahama golden sun rum
Orange slice for garnish
Maraschino cherry for garnish

Shake all liquids except the Tommy Bahama golden sun rum with ice. Strain into a glass over ice. Carefully float the dark rum on top. Garnish with the orange slice and Maraschino cherry.

Basil Hayden's Bubbly

1 oz. Basil Hayden's bourbon
Champagne to fill
Orange twist or Maraschino cherry for garnish

Pour the bourbon into a glass, and fill with champagne. Garnish with the orange twist or cherry.

Beach Baby

2 oz. Bailey's Irish cream
½ oz. Captain Morgan Parrot Bay coconut rum
Splash cream
Maraschino cherry for garnish
Chocolate syrup for garnish

Shake the first three ingredients vigorously with ice until foamy. Serve over ice in a rocks glass, and garnish with the cherry and chocolate syrup for a rich taste.

Beach Bum

1 oz. vodka
1½ oz. Midori melon liqueur
1 oz. cranberry juice

Shake with ice and strain into a cocktail glass. Serve straight up.

Beachcomber

1¼ oz. Smirnoff No. 21 vodka
¼ oz. Captain Morgan Parrot Bay coconut rum
½ oz. pineapple juice
Splash orange juice
2 orange slices for garnish

Pour the first four ingredients into a glass over ice, and stir well. Garnish with orange slices.

Belvedere Cytrus Chamomile Cooler "Boutique"

2 oz. Belvedere cytrus vodka
1 oz. honey
Dash egg white
1 oz. fresh chamomile tea, iced
½ oz. fresh lemon juice

Shake and pour into a rocks glass.

Belvedere Cytrus Chamomile Cooler "Casual"

2 oz. Belvedere cytrus vodka
½ oz. simple syrup (Dissolve 1 part sugar in 1 part boiling water. Let cool.)
2 oz. fresh chamomile tea, iced
½ fresh lemon juice
Splash Sprite
Orange twist for garnish

Build the first four ingredients in a highball glass. Top with a splash of Sprite, and garnish with the orange twist.

Belvedere Earl Grey Fizz

1 oz. Belvedere vodka
¾ oz. Earl Grey tea syrup
Moët et Chandon brut imperial champagne
Lemon twist for garnish

Shake the first two ingredients and strain into
a champagne flute. Top with the champagne.
Garnish with the lemon twist.

Belvedere Hot Pomegranate
Martini

1 small slice red chili, seeds removed
Dash simple syrup (Dissolve 1 part sugar in 1
    part boiling water. Let cool.)
2 oz. Belvedere pomaranzca vodka
½ oz. premium triple sec
¼ oz. fresh lemon juice
2 dashes grapefruit bitters
Orange slice for garnish
1 pink rose petal for garnish

Muddle the seeds and chili in a Boston glass
with simple syrup. Add the remaining ingredients, and shake with ice cubes. Strain into a
martini glass, and garnish with the orange slice
and pink rose petal.

Belvedere Pomaranzca Fizz

2 oz. Belvedere pomaranzca vodka
½ oz. fresh lemon juice
½ oz. simple syrup (Dissolve 1 part sugar in 1
    part boiling water. Let cool.)
Large orange twist for garnish

Shake the first three ingredients. Pour into a highball glass. Garnish with the large orange twist wrapped inside the glass.

Bermuda Rum Swizzle

2 oz. Gosling's black seal rum
1 oz. lime juice
1 oz. pineapple juice
1 oz. orange juice
¼ oz. Falernum
Orange slice for garnish
Maraschino cherry for garnish

Shake the first five ingredients with ice and strain into a highball glass over ice. Garnish with the orange slice and cherry.

Berry Fizz

2 oz. Alizé red passion
1 oz. strawberry vodka
2 oz. cranberry juice
Splash lemon-lime soda

Shake vigorously with ice. Strain into a martini glass, and serve straight up.

Berry Me in the Sand

3 fresh raspberries plus 2 extra for garnish
2 oz. SKYY Infusions raspberry vodka
1 oz. limoncello
2 oz. Prosecco
Lemon zest for garnish

Muddle 3 fresh raspberries in a pint glass. Add
ice, SKYY Infusions, and limoncello. Shake,
and strain into a champagne flute. Top with
Prosecco. Garnish with 2 raspberries on a pick
and a large lemon zest.

Berry Passionate Sangría

4 oz. Merlot
1½ oz. Stolichnaya razberi vodka
1½ oz. Hiram Walker blueberry passion
    schnapps
1 lemon squeeze
1 lime squeeze
1 orange squeeze
3 oz. lemon-lime soda

Build the first six ingredients in a 14-oz. glass
over ice. Pour into a shaker and back two
times to mix. Top with the lemon-lime soda.

Bikini Martini

1½ oz. Sagatiba pura cachaça
½ oz. limoncello
1 oz. fresh lemon juice
2 oz. passion fruit purée
½ oz. simple syrup (Dissolve 1 part sugar in 1
    part boiling water. Let cool.)
Slice passion fruit for garnish

Shake first five ingredients with ice and serve
in a martini glass. Garnish with a passion fruit
slice floating on top of the drink.

Bitter-Berry Lemonade

1½ oz. Smirnoff blueberry-flavored vodka
5 oz. bitter lemon soda
Blueberries for garnish

Build in a tall glass over ice. Garnish with the
blueberries.

Black and Four Fruits

1 oz. Bacardi black rum
1 oz. orange juice
1 oz. pineapple juice
1 oz. grapefruit juice
1 oz. lime juice

Pour the rum into a glass over ice. Add the
remaining ingredients, shake, and strain.

Blackberi Mambo

1 oz. Stolichnaya blakberi vodka
½ oz. Hiram Walker white peach schnapps
½ oz. Hiram Walker mango schnapps
1 oz. pineapple juice
1 oz. apple cider
¼ oz. fresh lime juice
Pineapple slice for garnish

Shake liquids over ice and strain into an old-fashioned glass. Garnish with the pineapple slice.

Black Iced Tea

¾ oz. orange juice
¾ oz. triple sec
¾ oz. brandy
¾ oz. Bacardi black rum
Juice ½ lime
Lime wedge for garnish
Coca-Cola Classic to top

Mix the first five ingredients in a tall glass over crushed ice. Stir well. Add the lime wedge, and top with the Coca-Cola.

Black Julep

10 mint leaves plus 1 mint sprig for garnish
1½ tsp. extra-fine sugar
2 splashes seltzer water
3 oz. José Cuervo black medallion tequila

Place the 10 mint leaves in the bottom of an old-fashioned glass or julep cup, and add the sugar. Crush with a muddler or wooden spoon until the leaves begin to come apart. Add a splash of seltzer. Fill the glass one-quarter full with crushed ice, and add the tequila. Top with another splash of seltzer, stir, and garnish with the mint sprig.

Bleu Breeze

3 oz. Alizé bleu
2 oz. pineapple juice
Pineapple wedge for garnish

Mix liquids together, and pour into a tall glass over ice. Garnish with the pineapple wedge.

Bleu Royale

1 oz. Alizé bleu
1 oz. vodka
2 oz. coconut rum
Splash club soda
Pineapple wedge for garnish

Mix liquids, and pour into a tall glass over ice. Garnish with the pineapple wedge.

Bloody Smurf

1½ oz. Stolichnaya 100-proof vodka
1 oz. Hiram Walker blueberry passion
    schnapps
3 oz. cranberry juice

Pour the first two ingredients into a Collins glass over ice. Add cranberry juice, and stir.

BLT

1¼ oz. Smirnoff blueberry-flavored vodka
½ oz. fortified white wine from cognac
½ oz. lemon juice
¼ oz. simple syrup (Dissolve 1 part sugar in 1
    part boiling water. Let cool.)

Build in a short glass over ice.

Blueberry Lemonade

2 oz. Hiram Walker blueberry passion
    schnapps
1 oz. Hiram Walker 60-proof triple sec
6 oz. lemonade
2 lemon twists and 2 lemon wedges for garnish

Pour half the schnapps and triple sec into a tumbler over ice; repeat. Fill each tumbler with the lemonade, and stir. Garnish each with a lemon twist and lemon wedge. Serves 2.

Blueberry Mango Mojito

1 oz. Malibu mango rum
1 oz. Hiram Walker blueberry passion
    schnapps
3 lime squeezes, plus 1 extra for garnish
6 fresh mint leaves
½ oz. simple syrup (Dissolve 1 part sugar in 1
    part boiling water. Let cool.)
1½ oz. soda
mint sprig for garnish

Shake the first five ingredients vigorously with
ice. Strain into a 14-oz. glass over ice. Top
with soda. Garnish with a lime squeeze and
the mint sprig.

Blueberry Martini

1 oz. blueberry schnapps
2 oz. Sauza blanco tequila

Serve straight up or on the rocks.

Blueberry Passion Cosmo

1½ oz. Stolichnaya citros vodka
1½ oz. Hiram Walker blueberry passion
    schnapps
2 oz. cranberry juice
¼ lime squeeze
Lime corkscrew for garnish

Shake the first four ingredients vigorously with
ice. Strain into a martini glass, and garnish with
a lime corkscrew.

Blueberry Passion Lemon Drop

Lemon juice to rim glass
Sugar to rim glass
2 oz. Stolichnaya citros vodka
1 oz. Hiram Walker blueberry passion
    schnapps
1½ oz. fresh lemon juice
½ oz. simple syrup (Dissolve 1 part sugar in 1
    part boiling water. Let cool.)
Lemon wheel for garnish

Rim a martini glass with lemon juice and sugar.
Shake the first two ingredients vigorously with
ice. Strain into the martini glass, and garnish
with the lemon.

Blueberry Passion Margarita

2 oz. Hiram Walker blueberry passion
    schnapps
1 oz. silver tequila
4 oz. sweet and sour mix (Dissolve 1 tsp. sugar
    in 3 oz. water. Add 2 oz. lemon juice.)
Fresh blueberries for garnish

Blend liquids with crushed ice until smooth.
Pour into a margarita glass, and garnish with
the blueberries.

Blueberry Passion Mojito

4–6 large mint leaves plus 1 extra for garnish
2 oz. white rum
1 oz. Hiram Walker blueberry passion
    schnapps
Juice 1 large lime
1 oz. soda
2 thin straws

Muddle the mint leaves in a Collins glass until
the essence is released. Fill the glass with ice.
Add the next three ingredients. Pour them into
a shaker, and pour back into the glass. Top
with the soda. Add 2 thin straws, and garnish
with the mint leaf.

Blueberry Popsicle

1 oz. Hiram Walker blueberry passion
    schnapps
2 oz. milk

Blend with ice and serve in a Collins glass.

Blueberry Sweet Tart

2 oz. white rum
2 oz. Hiram Walker blueberry passion
    schnapps
2 oz. fresh lime juice
Lime slice for garnish

Shake liquids with ice and strain into a martini
glass. Garnish with the lime slice.

Blue Dolphin

1 oz. Finlandia vodka
¼ oz. blue curaçao
¼ oz. Grand Marnier
1 oz. grapefruit juice
2 drops lime juice

Shake with ice. Serve over ice.

Blue-Eyed Boy

2 oz. SKYY vodka
1 oz. blue curaçao
Juice from ½ lime
3 oz. Sprite
Pear slice for garnish

Shake liquids and pour into a rocks glass over crushed ice. Garnish with the pear slice.

Blue Hawaiian

3 oz. Korbel brut or extra dry champagne
2 oz. pineapple juice
1 oz. blue curaçao

Pour the champagne into a champagne flute. Add the remaining ingredients.

Blue Haze

1 oz. Beefeater gin
1 oz. Hiram Walker blueberry passion
    schnapps
1 oz. ruby red grapefruit juice
⅓ oz. lemon-lime soda

Build in a highball glass over ice.

Blue Lagoon

¼ oz. Hiram Walker blue curaçao
1 oz. Stolichnaya vodka
1 oz. pineapple juice

Blend with ice, and serve.

Blue Lassi

4 oz. organic whole milk yogurt
1½ oz. Smirnoff blueberry-flavored vodka
1½ oz. whole milk
3 tbsp. sugar
1 tsp. rose flower water
1 green cardamom pod
½ apricot
Mint sprig for garnish

Blend the first seven ingredients with an immersion blender in a mixing bowl until smooth. Serve cold in a shot glass without ice as an apéritif. Garnish with the mint sprig.

Blue-Merang

1½ oz. Smirnoff blueberry-flavored vodka
8 seedless watermelon cubes
1 oz. fresh lime juice
¼ oz. simple syrup (Dissolve 1 part sugar in 1 part boiling water. Let cool.)
1 watermelon slice for garnish

Blend the first four ingredients with ice. Garnish with the watermelon slice.

Blue Sky

1½ oz. Canadian Mist
¾ oz. light rum
¾ oz. blue curaçao
6 oz. pineapple juice
8 oz. ice
Orange slice for garnish
Paper umbrella for decoration

Blend the first five ingredients until frozen.
Serve in a hurricane glass. Garnish with the
orange slice, and decorate with the umbrella.

Blushing White Peach Sangría

1 oz. white Zinfandel
1 oz. Hiram Walker white peach schnapps
1 oz. pineapple juice
2 oz. lemon-lime soda
2 slices fresh peach
4 pineapple chunks

Build the first three ingredients in a 14-oz.
glass over ice. Pour back and forth in a shaker
two times to mix, and top with lemon-lime
soda. Add the fruit, and serve.

Blusta

1½ oz. Smirnoff blueberry-flavored vodka
2 tsp. Grand Marnier
1 tsp. Maraschino liqueur
¼ oz. lemon juice
Sugar to rim glass
Whole lemon peel for garnish
Shake and serve straight up in a fizz/crusta glass rimmed with sugar. Garnish with an entire lemon peel.

Bombay Sapphire Tom Collins

2 oz. Bombay Sapphire gin
1 oz. fresh lemon juice
¾ oz. simple syrup (Dissolve 1 part sugar in 1
    part boiling water. Let cool.)
Club soda to top
Lemon wedge for garnish

Pour the first three ingredients into a Collins glass over ice, and stir well. Add more ice, and top with the club soda. Garnish with the lemon wedge.

Bring on the Funk

1½ oz. Smirnoff passion fruit-flavored vodka
1 oz. guava nectar
¼ oz. Maraschino liqueur
¼ oz. white vermouth (not dry)
3 dashes bitters
Lemon twist for garnish

Shake liquids with ice and strain into a martini glass. Garnish with the lemon twist.

Brown-Eyed Girl

1 tsp. Stirrings spiced apple rimmer garnish
2 oz. Stirrings pear martini mixer
1½ oz. Smirnoff vanilla vodka
Splash pineapple juice
Squeeze fresh lime juice

Rim a martini glass with the Stirrings garnish. Shake liquids vigorously with plenty of ice. Strain into the rimmed martini glass.

Bubble Gum

1 oz. cranberry vodka
¼ oz. peach schnapps
¼ oz. crème de bananes
1 oz. orange juice

Shake. Serve on the rocks.

Bushwacker

2 oz. Coco Lopez cream of coconut
2 oz. half-and-half
1 oz. Kahlúa
½ oz. dark crème de cacao
½ oz. rum

Blend with 1 cup ice until smooth.

Butterscotch Collins

1 tsp. sugar
½ oz. Drambuie
1½ oz. Dewar's White Label scotch
2 oz. lemon juice
1 oz. soda
Orange slice for garnish
Maraschino cherry for garnish

Dissolve sugar in 2 oz. water. Pour into a Collins glass over ice. Add Drambuie, scotch, and lemon juice, and stir. Top with the soda, and garnish with the orange slice and Maraschino cherry.

Café Cortado

1 oz. Marie Brizard coffee liqueur
1½ oz. half-and-half

Shake slowly over ice and pour into a rocks glass.

Cajun Martini

1¼ oz. Absolut Peppar
Dash extra-dry vermouth
Lemon twist or olive for garnish

Shake or stir the first two ingredients well over ice. Strain. Serve in a cocktail glass straight up or over ice. Garnish with the lemon twist or olive.

California Coastline

1 oz. Malibu coconut rum
1 oz. Marie Brizard peach liqueur
½ oz. Marie Brizard blue curaçao
2 oz. sweet and sour mix (Dissolve 1 tsp. sugar in 3 oz. water. Add 2 oz. lemon juice.)
2 oz. pineapple juice
Pineapple wedge for garnish

Blend liquids for 30 seconds. Pour into a glass over crushed ice, and garnish with the pineapple wedge.

Calypso Cool-Aid

1¼ oz. Rhum Barbancourt
1 oz. pineapple juice
½ oz. lemon or lime juice
¼ tsp. sugar
Soda to fill
Pineapple spear for garnish
Lime slice for garnish

Shake or blend the first four ingredients with ice, and pour into a tall glass. Fill with the soda, and garnish with the pineapple spear and lime slice.

Canton Ginger Mojito

2 fresh mint leaves
2 lime wedges
2 oz. Canton French ginger liqueur
½ oz. light rum
Soda to top

Muddle the fresh mint leaves and 2 lime wedges. Add the remaining ingredients, and serve in a tall glass over ice.

Canton Pimm's Cup

1 oz. Canton French ginger liqueur
1 oz. Pimm's No. 1 Cup
3 oz. ginger ale
1 orange slice
1 lemon slice
1 strawberry slice
1 cucumber slice
1 sprig mint

Serve in a tall glass over ice.

Cape Codder

1½ oz. Sobieski vodka
4 oz. cranberry juice
Club soda to fill
Orange slices for garnish

Build the first two ingredients in a Collins glass over ice cubes. Fill with club soda, and stir. Garnish with the orange slices.

Captain's Colada

1¼ oz. Captain Morgan spiced rum
1 oz. Coco Lopez cream of coconut
3 oz. pineapple juice
Pineapple spear for garnish

Blend liquids with ½ cup crushed ice. Garnish with the pineapple spear.

Captain's Daiquiri

1¼ oz. Captain Morgan original spiced rum
2 tsp. lime juice
½ tsp. sugar
Lime wedge for garnish

Shake or blend the first three ingredients with ice. Garnish with the lime wedge.

Captain's Morgarita

1½ oz. Captain Morgan original spiced rum
½ oz. Marie Brizard triple sec
6 oz. frozen limeade

Blend with 1 cup ice until smooth.

Caravella Limoncello Lemonade

1½ oz. EFFEN cherry vodka
1 oz. Caravella limoncello
2 oz. lemonade
Splash grenadine
Lemon peel for garnish
Maraschino cherry for garnish

Shake the first three ingredients with ice and pour into a tumbler glass. Add a splash of grenadine, and garnish with the lemon peel and Maraschino cherry.

Caribbean Champagne

¾ oz. light rum
¾ oz. crème de bananes
Chilled Korbel brut champagne to fill
Banana slice and/or Maraschino cherry for
    garnish

Pour the first two ingredients into a chilled
champagne glass. Fill with the champagne. Garnish with the banana slice and/or
Maraschino cherry.

Caribbean Colada

1½ oz. Hiram Walker Rhum Grandier
4 oz. pineapple juice
1½ oz. Coco Lopez cream of coconut
Pineapple spear for garnish

Blend the first three ingredients with cracked
ice until smooth, and garnish with the pineapple spear.

Chambuie

½ oz. Drambuie
3 oz. champagne

Pour the Drambuie into a champagne flute.
Top with the champagne.

Champagne Jubilee

1¼ oz. amaretto
½ oz. vodka
2 oz. cranberry juice
Chilled Korbel brut champagne to fill

Shake the first three ingredients and strain into a chilled champagne glass. Fill with the champagne.

Cherricane

1¾ oz. SKYY Infusions cherry vodka
3 oz. orange juice
2 oz. cranberry juice
1 oz. pineapple juice
⅛ oz. Midori melon liqueur

Shake the first four ingredients with ice. Pour into a hurricane or tall glass. Float the liqueur.

Cherries Jubilee

Sugar to rim glass
2 oz. SKYY Infusions cherry vodka
½ oz. Carolans Irish cream
½ oz. Cointreau
Maraschino cherry for garnish

Shake. Serve in a sugar-rimmed martini glass with the cherry garnish.

Cherry Chi-Chi

1¾ oz. SKYY Infusions cherry vodka
¾ oz. Coco Lopez cream of coconut
½ pineapple juice
¼ oz. heavy cream or milk

Blend with ice.

Cherry Cola

2 oz. SKYY Infusions cherry vodka
3 oz. cola
Maraschino cherry for garnish

Serve liquids in a tall glass over ice, and garnish
with the cherry.

Cherry Leader

1¾ oz. SKYY Infusions cherry vodka
3 oz. cranberry juice
1 oz. club soda

Serve in a tall glass.

Cherry Lifesaver

1½ oz. Laird's AppleJack
1½ oz. amaretto
1½ oz. cranberry juice
Maraschino cherry for garnish

Shake liquids vigorously with ice and strain into a martini glass. Garnish with the Maraschino cherry.

Cherry Patriot

1½ oz. SKYY Infusions cherry vodka
1 oz. fresh lemon juice
½ oz. Cointreau
½ oz. sweet vermouth
¾ oz. rye whiskey
2 oz. club soda
Lemon zest for garnish
Maraschino cherry for garnish

Shake liquids vigorously with ice. Strain into a tall pilsner-style glass. Garnish with the lemon zest and Maraschino cherry.

Cherry Picker

1½ oz. SKYY Infusions cherry vodka
3 oz. orange juice
½ oz. Campari

Pour the first two ingredients into a tall glass. Slowly pour the Campari down the center of the cocktail.

Cherry Ruvo

2 oz. SKYY Infusions cherry vodka
Dash grenadine
Cherry tomato for garnish
Slice pepperoni for garnish

Serve liquids in a chilled martini glass, and garnish with the tomato and pepperoni.

Cherry Stone

1 oz. SKYY Infusions cherry Vodka
½ oz. Frangelico liqueur or hazelnut liqueur
½ oz. Carolans Irish cream

Shake. Serve in a shot glass.

Chica Chica

1 oz. Sobieski vodka
¾ oz. Marie Brizard mango liqueur
½ oz. fresh lemon juice

Shake with ice, and strain into a martini glass.

Chi-Chi

1½ oz. Smirnoff vodka
1½ oz. coconut milk
1½ oz. pineapple juice
Pineapple chunk for garnish

Shake or blend liquids with ice, and garnish with the pineapple chunk.

Chocolate Passion Cream

¾ oz. Stolichnaya vanil vodka
¾ oz. Hiram Walker blueberry passion
   schnapps
¾ oz. Hiram Walker white crème de cacao
1 oz. half-and-half
Chocolate syrup to rim glass
Sugar to rim glass

Shake the first three ingredients vigorously with ice. Strain into a martini glass rimmed with chocolate and sugar.

Ci-Tea

2 oz. SKYY Infusions citrus vodka
2 oz. hot tea
Juice ½ lemon

Pour the first two ingredients into a hot cup. Add the lemon juice.

Citric Blast Tecate Light

6 oz. cold Tecate Light
6 oz. lemon-lime soda or lemonade
Sugar to rim glass

Mix liquids in a glass rimmed with sugar.
¡Salud!

Citron Cooler

1¼ oz. citron
½ oz. fresh lime juice
2 oz. tonic
Lime wedge for garnish

Pour the first two ingredients into a tall glass
over ice. Fill with the tonic. Garnish with the
lime wedge.

Citros Peach Fuzz

1 oz. Stolichnaya citros vodka
1 oz. Hiram Walker white peach schnapps
1 oz. half-and-half or heavy cream
Fresh peach slice for garnish

Blend liquids with crushed ice until smooth.
Pour into a hurricane glass, and garnish with
the peach slice.

Citrus in Provence

½ rosemary sprig, preferably organic, plus
    extra for garnish
½ oz. Meyer lemon juice
1½ oz. SKYY Infusions citrus vodka
½ oz. simple syrup (Dissolve 1 part sugar in 1
    part boiling water. Let cool.)
Dash soda

Muddle the ½ sprig of rosemary with the
lemon juice and simple syrup in a shaker.
Add ice and the vodka, and shake. Strain into
a rocks glass over ice, and top with the soda.
Garnish with the rosemary sprig.

Citrus Mist Colada

1½ oz. Canadian Mist
4½ oz. piña colada mix
2 oz. lemon-lime soda
Maraschino cherry for garnish
Lime slice for garnish

Blend liquids with ice cubes until thick. Serve in
an old-fashioned glass. Garnish with the cherry
and lime slice.

Citrus Supreme

4 oz. Gordon's citrus vodka
1 oz. Marie Brizard triple sec
1 (12-oz.) can frozen lemonade
2 cups lime- or lemon-flavored water

Blend with ice until slushy, and pour into a frozen long-stemmed bowl glass. Serves 2.

Classic Peach Daiquiri

1½ oz. Jubilee peach schnapps
1½ oz. sweet and sour mix (Dissolve 1 tsp.
    sugar in 3 oz. water. Add 2 oz. lemon juice.)
½ oz. triple sec
1 oz. rum

Blend with ice until smooth.

Classic Tiki Daiquiri

1½ oz. Stirrings simple margarita mixer
1½ oz. Oronoco rum
Squeeze lime juice

Shake the first two ingredients vigorously with ice. Strain into a rocks glass, and add the lime juice.

Cocoberry Pie

4 oz. Coco Lopez cream of coconut
3 oz. Hiram Walker blueberry passion
    schnapps
2 oz. half-and-half or heavy cream
Fresh blueberry for garnish

Blend liquids with crushed ice until smooth.
Pour into a Collins glass, and garnish with
the blueberry.

Coco Colada

1½ oz. dark crème de cacao
4 oz. pineapple juice
1½ oz. Coco Lopez cream of coconut
Pineapple spear for garnish

Blend liquids with ice until smooth, and garnish
with the pineapple spear.

Coco Lopez Shake

2½ oz. Coco Lopez cream of coconut
1 scoop vanilla ice cream

Blend with 1 cup ice until smooth.

Cocomotion

1½ oz. Puerto Rican dark rum
4 oz. Coco Lopez cream of coconut
2 oz. lime juice

Blend liquids with 1½ cups ice, and serve in a margarita glass.

Coconut Punch

1¼ oz. Bacardi or Bacardi Gold/Oro rum
2 oz. Coco Lopez cream of coconut
½ oz. lemon juice
3–4 tbsp. vanilla ice cream

Shake or blend with crushed ice, and pour into a tall glass.

Comfort Colada

1½ oz. Southern Comfort
1 oz. Coco Lopez cream of coconut
2 oz. pineapple juice
1–2 Maraschino cherries for garnish

Blend liquids with 1 or 2 crushed ice cubes until ice is completely broken up and liquid is frothy. Serve in a tall glass over ice, and garnish with the cherries.

Comfort Wallbanger

1 oz. Southern Comfort
½ oz. Galliano
Orange juice to fill

Build in a tall glass over ice cubes. Stir.

Cool Heaven

¼ oz. Sobieski vodka
1½ oz. Marie Brizard Manzanita
½ oz. club soda
¾ oz. fruit juice of your choice

Shake with ice and strain into a cocktail glass.

Corzo Grand Margarita

Salt to rim glass
3 oz. Corzo silver tequila
1 oz. Grand Marnier
Dash fresh lime juice
2 oz. pineapple juice
Pineapple slice for garnish

Salt half the rim of a martini glass. Shake liquids vigorously and strain into the martini glass. Garnish with the pineapple slice.

Cosmo Royale

4 oz. champagne
½ oz. Cointreau
½ oz. vodka
½ oz. cranberry juice
Orange twist for garnish

Build in a champagne glass. Garnish with the orange twist.

Cow Shot

1½ oz. Southern Comfort
½ oz. crème de cacao
3 oz. cold milk

Pour into an 8-oz. glass over ice, and stir.

Cream Soda

1¼ oz. Captain Morgan original spiced rum
¼ oz. triple sec
1 oz. lime juice
2 oz. pineapple juice
Lemon slice for garnish

Pour liquids into a tall glass over ice. Stir well, and garnish with the lemon slice.

Crown Fizz

1½ oz. Crown Royal Special Reserve
1½ oz. lemon juice
6 oz. club soda
4 tsp. sugar
Lemon slice for garnish

Shake liquids and strain into a tall glass over ice. Garnish with the lemon slice.

Crown Manhattan

1 oz. Crown Royal Special Reserve
¼ oz. sweet vermouth
Dash bitters
Maraschino cherry for garnish

Stir liquids with ice, and strain into a chilled cocktail glass or serve on the rocks in an old-fashioned glass. Garnish with the Maraschino cherry.

Crown of Roses

1 oz. Crown Royal Special Reserve
½ oz. amaretto
1 oz. pineapple juice
¼ oz. cranberry juice
3 dashes Angostura bitters
Maraschino cherry for garnish

Shake with ice and strain into a chilled cocktail glass. Garnish with the Maraschino cherry.

Crown Royal Special Reserve Martini

1 oz. Crown Royal Special Reserve
½ oz. Grand Marnier

Stir with ice, and strain into a chilled cocktail glass.

Crown Sidecar

Sugar to rim glass
1 oz. Crown Royal Special Reserve
¼ oz. triple sec
2 oz. sweet and sour mix (Dissolve 1 tsp. sugar in 3 oz. water. Add 2 oz. lemon juice.)
Lime wedge for garnish

Sugar the rim of a chilled cocktail glass. Shake liquids with ice and strain into the cocktail glass. Garnish with the lime wedge.

Cruzan Coral Reef

1 oz. Cruzan guava rum
1 oz. Cruzan coconut rum
1 oz. pink grapefruit juice
Grapefruit wedge for garnish

Shake with ice, and strain into a tumbler over fresh ice. Garnish with the grapefruit wedge.

Cucumber Melon Cosmo

2 oz. Stirrings watermelon martini mixer
1½ oz. citrus-flavored vodka or gin
English cucumber slices for garnish
Watermelon slices for garnish

Shake and serve with the thin slices of English cucumber and watermelon.

Cuervo Acapulco Fizz

1½ oz. José Cuervo Especial tequila
1½ oz. cream
2 oz. orange juice
2 tsp. sugar
2 dashes orange bitters
1 egg
Orange slice for garnish

Blend the first six ingredients with 3 ice cubes. Pour into a highball glass, and garnish with the orange slice.

Cuervo Raspberry Margarita

1½ oz. José Cuervo Especial tequila
1 oz. triple sec
1 oz. Major Peters' sweetened West Indian
    lime juice
½ cup raspberries plus extra for garnish

Blend liquids, ½ cup raspberries, and ½ cup ice until frothy, and garnish with raspberries.

Cuervo Sunrise

1.5 oz. José Cuervo Especial tequila
3 oz. orange juice
½ oz. grenadine
Maraschino cherry for garnish

Pour the tequila into a tall highball glass over ice. Fill with the orange juice, leaving a little room on top to stir. Slowly pour in the grenadine. Garnish with the cherry.

Deep Passion

1½ oz. Stolichnaya citros vodka
1½ oz. Malibu mango rum
1½ oz. Hiram Walker blueberry passion
    schnapps
2 oz. sweet and sour mix (Dissolve 1 tsp.
    sugar in 3 oz. water. Add 2 oz. lemon
    juice.)
2 oz. ginger ale
2 oz. soda
1 scoop lemon or rainbow sherbet

Build the first six ingredients in a 14-oz. glass over ice. Top with the scoop of sherbet. Makes 2 cocktails.

DeKuyper Peachtree Margarita

1 oz. DeKuyper luscious peachtree schnapps
2 oz. Sauza tequila
½ oz. DeKuyper signature triple sec
3 oz. sweet and sour mix (Dissolve 1 tsp. sugar
   in 3 oz. water. Add 2 oz. lemon juice.)

Blend with ice.

Dewar's and Ginger Beer

1 oz. Dewar's White Label scotch
3 oz. ginger beer
Orange wedge for garnish

Pour the scotch into a glass over ice. Top with
the ginger beer, and garnish with the orange
wedge.

Dip in the Ocean

1 oz. Tommy Bahama golden sun rum
½ oz. Midori melon liqueur
½ oz. coconut rum
Splash orange juice
Splash pineapple juice
Splash cranberry juice
Splash grenadine
Pineapple slice for garnish
Orange slice for garnish

Serve liquids over ice in a short glass. Garnish
with the pineapple and orange slices.

Dirty Banana

2 scoops vanilla ice cream plus more as
    needed
1 oz. Hiram Walker crème de bananes
1 oz. Hiram Walker white crème de cacao
1 oz. Kahlúa

Blend 6 ice cubes and the ice cream until
smooth. Add the liqueurs. Add more ice cream
to achieve a milk shake-like consistency.

Dirty Olive

¾ oz. Sauza blanco tequila
¼ oz. black olive juice
Black olive for garnish

Serve over ice, and garnish with the olive.

Disarita Margarita

1 oz. José Cuervo 1800 tequila
½ oz. Disaronno amaretto
3 oz. margarita mix
½ cup crushed ice
Lime slice for garnish

Blend liquids with ice. Garnish with the lime.

Do Ask, Do Tell

2 oz. SKYY vodka
2 oz. lemonade
2 oz. 7-Up
Star fruit slice for garnish

Mix in a shaker with ice. Serve in a rocks glass.
Garnish with the slice of star fruit.

Double SKYY Transfusion

1½ oz. SKYY Infusions grape vodka
3 oz. grape juice

Serve in a tall glass over ice.

Dreamsicle

1½ oz. Hiram Walker orchard orange
    schnapps
3 oz. vanilla ice cream

Blend until smooth.

Dundee

2 tsp. Drambuie
1½ oz. Bombay dry gin
2 tbsp. Dewar's White Label scotch
1 tsp. lemon juice
Maraschino cherry for garnish
Lemon twist for garnish
Shake with ice and strain into a rocks glass. Add ice. Garnish with the cherry and lemon twist.

Electric Lemonade

1 oz. Sobieski vodka
½ oz. Hiram Walker orange curaçao
4 oz. lemonade
½ tbsp. puréed strawberries
Lemon wheel for garnish

Blend the first four ingredients with ice. Serve in a hurricane glass, and garnish with the lemon wheel.

Electric Peach

1 oz. Finlandia vodka
¼ oz. peach schnapps
½ oz. cranberry juice cocktail
¼ oz. orange juice

Serve on the rocks or straight up.

Electric Tickler

½ oz. Drambuie
1½ oz. Bombay dry gin
¼ oz. Martini & Rossi Rosso vermouth
2 oz. orange juice
Club soda to fill
Lemon wedge for garnish

Shake the first four ingredients in a Collins glass with ice. Strain into a glass over ice. Fill with the soda. Garnish with the lemon wedge.

Emerald Isle

¾ shot Tullamore Dew
¾ shot green crème de menthe
2 scoops vanilla ice cream
Soda water to fill

Blend the first three ingredients, and add the soda water. Stir.

Enchanted 360

1 oz. 360 vodka
½ oz. hazelnut liqueur
½ oz. Irish cream liqueur
1 oz. half-and-half

Shake or blend with ice. Serve in a chilled martini glass or over ice.

Firecracker

6 fresh pomegranate seeds and juice
2 shots Cabo Wabo tequila reposado
¼ oz. simple syrup (Dissolve 1 part sugar in 1
    part boiling water. Let cool.)
1 oz. fresh passion fruit (available at gourmet
    shops)

Muddle pomegranate seeds and juice in a
shaker. Add the remaining ingredients, shake
with ice, and strain through a fine-mesh strainer
into a chilled glass.

Flamingo

1 oz. Beefeater gin
2 oz. pineapple juice
1 oz. Coco Lopez cream of coconut
1 oz. sweet and sour mix (Dissolve 1 tsp. sugar
    in 3 oz. water. Add 2 oz. lemon juice.)

Blend with crushed ice until smooth. Strain
    into a chilled glass.

Florida Banana Lopez

2 oz. Coco Lopez cream of coconut
4 oz. orange juice
1 medium banana

Blend with 1 cup ice until smooth.

For Grape's Sake

1½ oz. SKYY Infusions grape vodka
1½ oz. Zen green tea liqueur

Shake. Serve on the rocks.

Fountain of Youth

1½ oz. Smirnoff blueberry-flavored vodka
1½ oz. Stirrings pomegranate martini mixer
Splash açai juice
Dried goji berries for garnish
Blueberries for garnish

Serve over ice, and garnish with goji berries
and blueberries. (Note: Açai juice and goji
berries are sold at health food stores.)

French Martini

1½ oz. Sobieski vodka
1 oz. pineapple juice
1 oz. Marie Brizard raspberry liqueur

Shake and strain into a martini glass.

Fresh

1 oz. Sauza blanco tequila
1½ oz. lemon-lime soda
Squeeze lime wedge

Serve over ice.

Fresh Peach Tini

2 oz. Stolichnaya citros vodka
½ oz. Hiram Walker white peach schnapps
½ oz. sweet and sour mix (Dissolve 1 tsp.
   sugar in 3 oz. water. Add 2 oz. lemon
   juice.)
2 oz. cranberry juice
Frozen peach slice for garnish

Shake liquids vigorously with ice. Strain into a
martini glass. Garnish with the peach slice.

Frozen Apple Lemonade

1 oz. DeKuyper pucker sour apple schnapps
1 oz. Absolut vodka
1 oz. lemonade

Blend with ice, and serve in a tall glass.

Frozen Melon Madness

1 oz. DeKuyper luscious melon dew schnapps
1 oz. DeKuyper watermelon squeeze
   schnapps
1 oz. rum
1 oz. sweet and sour mix (Dissolve 1 tsp. sugar
   in 3 oz. water. Add 2 oz. lemon juice.)
Splash lemon-lime soda

Blend with ice.

Frozen Tropical Split

1¼ oz. Malibu tropical banana rum
¾ oz. Hiram Walker white crème de cacao
1 oz. strawberry purée
2 oz. piña colada mix
Strawberry slice for garnish
Banana slice for garnish

Blend liquids with 1 cup ice until smooth.
Garnish with the strawberry and banana slice.

Fruit Salad

1½ oz. DeKuyper pucker cherry
½ oz. DeKuyper pucker grape
½ oz. DeKuyper luscious peachtree schnapps
Splash orange juice

Combine and serve as a shot or mixed drink.

Fruity Russian

1 oz. Stolichnaya ohranj vodka
1 oz. Kahlúa
1 oz. Hiram Walker mango schnapps

Mix, and serve over ice in a rocks glass.

Fuzzless Screwdriver

1½ oz. Jubilee peach schnapps
1 oz. Sobieski vodka
2 oz. orange juice

Blend with ice until smooth.

Fuzzy Monkey Martini

1 oz. Stolichnaya vodka
½ oz. Malibu coconut rum
1 oz. Hiram Walker white peach schnapps
1 oz. cranberry juice
Pineapple slice for garnish

Shake with ice, and strain into a martini glass.
Garnish with the pineapple slice.

Georgia Peach

1½ oz. DeKuyper luscious peachtree
   schnapps
¾ oz. DeKuyper crème de cocoa light
1 oz. cream
Peach wheel for garnish

Shake liquids and strain into a cocktail glass.
Garnish with the peach wheel.

Get in Grape Shape

2 oz. SKYY Infusions grape vodka
1 oz. Lillet Blanc apéritif wine
2 oz. pineapple juice
1 oz. fresh lime juice
1 oz. simple syrup (Dissolve 1 part sugar in 1
   part boiling water. Let cool.)
Fresh grapes on a toothpick for garnish

Shake liquids vigorously with ice. Strain into
a stemless champagne flute. Garnish with
the grapes.

Gimme More

2 oz. SKYY vodka
½ oz. triple sec
3 oz. strawberry-mango juice
Strawberry for garnish

Shake with ice. Serve in a rocks glass. Garnish
with the strawberry.

Ginger Cherry Blossom

4 fresh or 6 frozen black cherries
Splash cranberry juice
2 oz. Canton French ginger liqueur
½ oz. Sobieski vodka

Muddle the black cherries and splash of cranberry juice. Add the liqueur and vodka. Serve in a chilled martini glass.

Ginger Lime Sorbet

¼ oz. fresh white ginger
1½ oz. rum
1½ oz. Stirrings pear martini
1 oz. Stirrings strawberry daiquiri
Lime wedge for garnish

Muddle the white ginger. Add the remaining ingredients, shake, and strain into a glass over ice. Garnish with the lime wedge.

Ginger Margarita

2 oz. Canton French ginger liqueur
½ oz. silver tequila
½ oz. fresh lime juice
Splash orange juice

Serve in a rocks glass over ice, or blend with ice and serve in a margarita glass.

Ginger Rose Martini

2 oz. Alizé rose
Splash ginger ale
Strawberry slice for garnish

Pour the Alizé rose into a shaker over ice, and chill. Shake. Strain into a martini glass. Top with ginger ale, and garnish with the strawberry slice.

G'intastic Garden

1 strawberry, quartered, plus 1 strawberry, halved, for garnish
2 basil leaves plus basil sprig for garnish
½ lime
½ oz. agave nectar or simple syrup (Dissolve 1 part sugar in 1 part boiling water. Let cool.)
1½ oz. G'vine gin
1 oz. white grape juice

Muddle the first four ingredients in a shaker. Add the gin, white grape juice, and ice. Shake and serve in a cocktail glass. Garnish with half a strawberry and the basil sprig.

G'intriguing

½ oz. agave nectar or simple syrup (Dissolve 1
     part sugar in 1 part boiling water. Let cool.)
2 slices cucumber plus 1 slice extra for garnish
5 cilantro leaves
1 lime wedge
1½ oz. G'vine gin
1 oz. tonic

Muddle the first four ingredients in a shaker.
Add the gin, tonic, and ice. Shake, and serve in a
highball glass. Garnish with the cucumber slice.

Godiva Chocolate Berry Diva

1 oz. Godiva milk chocolate liqueur
1 oz. raspberry liqueur
4 oz. club soda

Pour the first two ingredients into a glass over
ice, and top with the club soda.

Go Green, Be Mary

1½ oz. 360 vodka
3½ oz. bloody Mary mix
2 dashes Tabasco
Squeeze lemon wedge
Celery stalk for garnish
Lemon wedge for garnish

Pour liquids into a glass, garnish with the celery stalk and lemon wedge, and serve.

Golden Delicious

2 oz. Alizé gold passion
1 oz. apple schnapps
½ oz. vodka
½ oz. triple sec

Shake vigorously with ice, strain, and serve straight up in a martini glass.

Golden Mango

1 oz. Martell cognac
1 oz. Hiram Walker mango schnapps
Splash ginger ale
Lime wedge for garnish

Serve liquids in a rocks glass, and garnish with the lime wedge.

Golden Pear

1 oz. Martell cognac
1 oz. Hiram Walker pear schnapps
Splash ginger ale
Lime wedge for garnish

Serve liquids in a rocks glass, and garnish with the lime wedge.

Gordon's China Clipper Cooler

1½ oz. Gordon's gin
3 oz. club soda
3 oz. cranberry juice
Maraschino cherry for garnish
Pineapple spear for garnish

Fill stemmed glass with ice cubes. Add the gin, club soda, and cranberry juice. Stir, and garnish with the cherry and pineapple spear.

Gordon's Limelight Cooler

2 oz. Gordon's gin
1 oz. lime juice
4 oz. wine cooler or seltzer water
Lime wedge for garnish

Pour the first two ingredients into a tall glass over ice. Fill with the wine cooler or seltzer water. Garnish with the lime wedge.

Gordon's Orange Blossom Cooler

1½ oz. Gordon's gin
3 oz. club soda
Orange juice to fill
Orange slice for garnish

Pour liquids into a tall glass over ice. Garnish with the orange slice.

Gordon's Silver Bullet Cooler

1½ oz. Gordon's gin
1 oz. lime juice
6 oz. tonic
Lime slice for garnish

Pour the first two ingredients into a tall glass over ice. Fill with the tonic, stir gently, and garnish with the lime slice.

Gordon's Trade Wind Cooler

1½ oz. Gordon's gin
3 oz. club soda
3 oz. pineapple juice
Orange slice for garnish

Fill a tall glass with ice cubes. Add the gin, club soda, and pineapple juice. Stir, and garnish with the orange slice.

Gordon's Tropical Paradise Cooler

1½ oz. Gordon's gin
3 oz. club soda
3 oz. fruit punch
Pineapple spear for garnish

Pour liquids into a stemmed glass over ice. Stir, and garnish with the pineapple spear.

Grape Crush

1 oz. Sobieski vodka
1 oz. black raspberry liqueur
2 oz. sweet and sour mix (Dissolve 1 tsp.
    sugar in 3 oz. water. Add 2 oz. lemon
    juice.)
1 oz. 7-Up
Orange slice or Maraschino cherry for garnish

Pour liquids over ice in a Collins glass. Garnish
with the orange slice or cherry.

Grape Fruits

1 oz. SKYY Infusions grape vodka
1 oz. SKYY Infusions citrus vodka
1 oz. cranberry juice

Shake. Serve in a tall glass over ice.

Grape Hopper

1 oz. SKYY Infusions grape vodka
1 oz. Carolans Irish cream
½ oz. green crème de menthe

Shake. Serve in a chilled martini glass or on
the rocks.

Grapeshot

1¾ oz. SKYY Infusions grape vodka
¾ oz. Midori melon liqueur

Shake and serve on the rocks.

Grass Skirt

1 oz. Tanqueray London dry gin
1 oz. pineapple juice
½ tsp. grenadine
¼ oz. triple sec
Pineapple slice for garnish

Shake the first three ingredients vigorously with ice. Pour into an old-fashioned glass. Garnish with the pineapple slice.

Green Appletini

1 oz. Smirnoff green apple vodka
Splash sweet and sour mix (Dissolve 1 tsp. sugar in 3 oz. water. Add 2 oz. lemon juice.)
Splash apple schnapps
Apple slice for garnish

Shake liquids and strain into a martini glass. Garnish with the apple slice.

Green Bomb

1 oz. Jägermeister liqueur
1 oz. Hiram Walker pear schnapps

Chill and serve in a shot glass.

Green Hornet

1 oz. Finlandia vodka
¼ oz. Midori melon liqueur
½ oz. sweet and sour mix (Dissolve 1 tsp.
    sugar in 3 oz. water. Add 2 oz. lemon juice.)

Shake with ice. Serve over ice or in a chilled
martini glass.

Green James

1 oz. Jameson Irish whiskey
1½ oz. Hiram Walker pear schnapps
¼ oz. lime juice
Lime wedge for garnish

Shake liquids and strain into a martini glass.
Garnish with the lime wedge.

Green Lemonade

1½ oz. SKYY Infusions citrus vodka
1 oz. Midori melon liqueur
2 oz. club soda
Lemon rind circle for garnish

Serve liquids in a tall glass, and garnish with the lemon rind circle.

G'Spot

1½ oz. G'vine gin
½ oz. Chambord
½ oz. simple syrup (Dissolve 1 part sugar in 1 part boiling water. Let cool.)
½ oz. fresh lime juice
½ oz. fresh lemon juice
Lime wheel for garnish
Lemon twist for garnish

Shake with ice and strain into a martini glass. Garnish with the lime wheel and lemon twist.

Guava Good Time

1½ oz. Cruzan guava rum
2 oz. mango juice
1 oz. apricot juice
Fruit slice of your choice for garnish

Shake liquids with ice and strain into a highball glass over ice. Garnish with a slice of fruit.

G'Vine Orchid

1½ oz. G'Vine gin
1½ oz. pink grapefruit juice
½ oz. Monin elderflower syrup
1½ oz. brut champagne
Orchid for garnish

Shake the first three ingredients with ice, and add the champagne so that it mixes with the rest of the ingredients. Pour into a highball glass, and garnish with the orchid.

Halo

2 oz. SKYY Infusions citrus vodka
3 oz. club soda
Lemon rind circle for garnish

Serve liquids in a tall glass, and garnish with the lemon rind circle, like a halo.

Heat Wave

4 oz. orange juice
1½ oz. Bacardi superior rum

Blend with ½ cup ice until smooth. Serve in a 10-oz. glass.

Herradura Margarita

1 oz. Herradura silver tequila
½ oz. Tuaca
½ oz. Chambord
1½ oz. lime juice
1½ oz. simple syrup (Dissolve 1 part sugar in
    1 part boiling water. Let cool.)
Lime wedge for garnish

Shake liquids with ice and strain into a rocks
glass over ice. Garnish with the lime wedge.

Herradura Splash

1¼ oz. Herradura silver tequila
2 oz. pineapple juice
2 oz. cranberry juice
Splash lemon-lime soda

Shake with ice and serve over ice.

Hibiscus

2 oz. Korbel brut or extra dry champagne
2 oz. Ocean Spray cranberry juice
Frozen strawberries for garnish

Pour the champagne into a large champagne
flute. Slowly stir in the cranberry juice. Garnish
with the strawberries.

Honolulu Cooler

Juice ½ lime
1½ oz. Southern Comfort
Hawaiian pineapple juice to fill

Build in a tall glass over crushed ice.

Hot Lips

1 oz. Finlandia vodka
¼ oz. Goldschläger schnapps

Serve in a chilled shot glass.

Hula Hoop

1 oz. Finlandia vodka
1 oz. pineapple juice
½ oz. orange juice

Shake with ice. Serve in a rocks glass over ice.

Icy Mango

1 oz. Beefeater gin
1 oz. Hiram Walker mango schnapps
¼ oz. lemon or lime juice
Dash bitters
Lemon wedge for garnish

Shake liquids and strain into a martini glass.
Garnish with the lemon wedge.

Icy Pink

1 oz. Beefeater gin
1 oz. Hiram Walker grapefruit schnapps
¼ oz. fresh lemon or lime juice
Dash bitters
Lemon wedge for garnish

Shake liquids and strain into a martini glass.
Garnish with the lemon wedge.

Independence Daisy

5 fresh raspberries plus extra for garnish
5 fresh blueberries plus extra for garnish
1 tbsp. sugar
2 oz. Knob Creek bourbon
1 oz. DeKuyper triple sec
6 mint sprigs
Splash DeKuyper pucker raspberry schnapps
Mint leaf for garnish

Muddle the fruit with the sugar in an old-fashioned glass, and add the next four ingredients. Garnish with the berries and mint leaf.

Irish Iced Tea

4 oz. strong, warm tea or iced-tea mix
1 tsp. sugar
1½ oz. Irish whiskey
Lemon slice, orange slice, or mint sprig for
  garnish

Pour the sugar and warm tea into a glass over
plenty of ice. Stir until sugar is dissolved. Add
the Irish whiskey, and garnish with the lemon
or orange slice or mint sprig.

Island Pleasure

1 oz. DeKuyper crème de bananes
½ oz. Frangelico
2 oz. cream
1½ oz. Angostura grenadine
Pineapple slice for garnish
Maraschino cherry on an umbrella for garnish

Blend the first four ingredients with crushed
ice. Serve in a 12-oz. glass. Spear the pineapple slice and cherry on a paper umbrella
for garnish.

It Ain't Easy Being Green

1¼ oz. 360 vodka
¾ oz. green crème de menthe
¾ oz. chocolate liqueur
1 oz. half-and-half

Shake or blend with ice. Serve on the rocks or in a chilled martini glass.

Jack Rose

1½ oz. Laird's AppleJack
1 oz. fresh lemon juice
½ oz. grenadine

Shake vigorously with ice. Strain into a chilled martini glass.

Jameson Whirlaway

2 oz. Jameson Irish whiskey
1 oz. Hiram Walker white peach schnapps
Dash bitters
Splash club soda

Mix the first three ingredients with cracked ice. Pour into a tumbler, and top with the club soda.

Jamie Blue

1 oz. Jameson Irish whiskey
1 oz. Hiram Walker blueberry passion
   schnapps

Mix with cracked ice. Pour into a rocks glass
and enjoy!

Jersey Girl

1½ oz. Laird's AppleJack
1 oz. Cointreau
½ oz. fresh lime juice
2 dashes cranberry juice
Lime wedge for garnish

Shake liquids vigorously with ice. Strain into
a chilled martini glass. Garnish with the lime
wedge.

Jewel

1 oz. 1800 select silver tequila
¼ oz. white cranberry juice
¼ oz. Cointreau
Dash port

Combine the first three ingredients, and freeze
for at least six hours. Pour into a frozen martini
glass. Using an eye dropper or syringe, add
5–6 drops of the port into the frozen glass. The
port will freeze and fall slowly to the bottom,
lightly coloring the drink and dissolving as the
drink warms.

Jim Beam Black Cherry

1½ oz. Jim Beam black bourbon
¾ oz. Cruzan black cherry rum
Lemon-lime soda to top

Build over ice in a tall highball glass.

Juicy Basil Hayden's

1¼ oz. Basil Hayden's bourbon
½ oz. DeKuyper triple sec
Splash orange juice
Splash cranberry juice
Splash simple syrup (Dissolve 1 part sugar in
    1 part boiling water. Let cool.)

Build over ice.

Jungle Fever

3 oz. DeKuyper harvest pear schnapps
Splash pineapple juice
Maraschino cherry for garnish

Pour the schnapps into a glass over ice. Add the
pineapple juice, and garnish with the cherry.

Kahlúa Banana

1½ oz. Kahlúa
¾ oz. rum
2 oz. pineapple juice
2 oz. Coco Lopez cream of coconut
Fresh banana

Blend with ice.

Kahlúa Banana Cream Fizz

⅓ oz. Kahlúa
⅓ oz. rum
⅓ oz. crème de bananes
Cream or milk to top

Blend the first three ingredients. Pour into a glass, and top with the cream or milk.

Kahlúa Colada

1½ oz. Kahlúa
2 oz. Coco Lopez cream of coconut
2 oz. pineapple juice

Blend with ice.

Kentucky Lemonade

Sugar to rim glass
1½ oz. Knob Creek bourbon
¾ oz. limoncello
2 oz. sweet and sour mix (Dissolve 1 tsp.
   sugar in 3 oz. water. Add 2 oz. lemon
   juice.)
¼ oz. simple syrup (Dissolve 1 part sugar in 1
   part boiling water. Let cool.)
3–5 mint leaves
Lemon slice for garnish

Rim a cocktail glass with sugar, and chill it. Shake
the next five ingredients with ice. Strain into the
cocktail glass. Garnish with the lemon slice.

Kentucky Margarita

1¼ oz. Jim Beam bourbon
Splash DeKuyper triple sec
Splash sweet and sour mix (Dissolve 1 tsp.
   sugar in 3 oz. water. Add 2 oz. lemon
   juice.)

Shake with ice. Serve over ice.

Key West Song

1¼ oz. Captain Morgan original spiced rum
1 oz. Coco Lopez cream of coconut
2 oz. orange juice

Blend with ice until smooth.

Kiwi Drop

1½ oz. Stirrings lemon drop cocktail mixer
1½ oz. Smirnoff citrus vodka
Kiwi slice for garnish

Mix liquids with ice, and strain into a martini glass over the kiwi slice.

Kiwi Lime Frozen Colada

2 bottles José Cuervo margarita mix
½ cup José Cuervo Especial tequila
2 kiwis, peeled and cubed
Juice and zest 1 lime
2 tbsp. honey
½ cup coconut milk
Kiwi or lime wheel for garnish

Blend the first six ingredients until smooth, and pour into a goblet. Garnish with a kiwi or a lime slice. Serves 2.

Knuckle-Buster

½ oz. Drambuie
1½ oz. Dewar's White Label scotch
1 tsp. Bacardi 151 rum

Pour into an old-fashioned glass over ice. Stir.

Korbel Royale

2 tsp. Chambord
1 oz. Korbel brandy
5 oz. Korbel champagne

Slowly stir the first two ingredients in a large champagne flute. Top with the champagne.

Krush

3 oz. Korbel champagne
2 oz. DeKuyper raspberry rush
Frozen raspberries for garnish

Serve liquids in a glass with shaved ice, and garnish with the raspberries.

Laser Disk

½ oz. Drambuie
½ oz. Dewar's White Label scotch
½ oz. lemonade

Shake. Serve in a shot glass.

Lemon Chiffon

1 oz. Finlandia vodka
¼ oz. triple sec
1 oz. sweet and sour mix (Dissolve 1 tsp. sugar
    in 3 oz. water. Add 2 oz. lemon juice.)
Fresh lemon wedge for garnish

Pour liquids into a glass. Squeeze the lemon,
and drop into the glass.

Lemon Meringue SKYY

Lemon to rim glass
1½ oz. SKYY Infusions citrus vodka
½ oz. Carolans Irish cream

Rim a martini glass with lemon, and chill.
Shake liquids with ice. Pour the mix into the
martini glass.

Lez Is More

1½ oz. SKYY vodka
1 oz. crème de menthe
1 oz. Baileys Irish cream
Orange peel curl for garnish

Shake with ice. Strain into a martini glass.
Garnish with the orange peel curl.

Limoncello Martini

1½ oz. vodka
½ oz. Caravella limoncello
Lemon peel for garnish

Shake liquids with ice. Pour into a martini
glass. Garnish with the lemon peel.

London Fog #1

1 oz. Beefeater gin
1 oz. Hiram Walker blueberry passion
   schnapps
2 oz. ruby red grapefruit juice
Lemon twist for garnish

Shake liquids with ice and strain into a martini
glass. Garnish with the lemon twist.

London Fog #2

2 oz. Beefeater gin
1½ oz. Hiram Walker blueberry passion
   schnapps
4 oz. sweet and sour mix (Dissolve 1 tsp.
   sugar in 3 oz. water. Add 2 oz. lemon
   juice.)
1 oz. cola
Lemon squeeze for garnish

Shake the first three ingredients vigorously with
ice. Strain into a 14-oz. glass over ice. Top with
1 oz. cola. Garnish with the lemon squeeze.

L'Orientale

1 oz. Canton French ginger liqueur
1 oz. vodka
¼ oz. Chambord
¼ oz. orange juice

Serve in a chilled martini glass.

Love Bite

4 oz. Korbel Chardonnay champagne
4 oz. Red Bull
2 oz. Finlandia vodka

Stir in a tall glass.

Lychee Royale

4 oz. sparkling wine
½ oz. 1800 tequila
½ oz. SOHO lychee liqueur
½ oz. raspberry liqueur
Sparkling wine or champagne to top

Combine the first four ingredients, and pour into a champagne flute. Top with sparkling wine or champagne.

Malibu Mango Kamikaze

1¾ oz. Malibu mango rum
1 oz. Stolichnaya citrus vodka
½ oz. Hiram Walker triple sec
¾ oz. fresh lime juice
Lime slice for garnish

Shake liquids and strain into a tall glass over ice. Garnish with the lime slice.

Malibu Orange Colada

1½ oz. Malibu coconut rum
1 oz. triple sec
4 oz. piña colada mix

Blend with ice until smooth.

Malibu Passion Tea

1 oz. Malibu passion fruit rum
2 oz. iced tea
1 oz. lemon-lime soda
Lime slice for garnish

Serve liquids over ice in a tall glass, and garnish with the lime slice.

Malibu Pineapple Cosmo

1½ oz. Malibu pineapple rum
¾ oz. Hiram Walker triple sec
¾ oz. fresh lime juice
¾ oz. cranberry juice
Lime slice for garnish

Shake and strain into a martini glass. Garnish with the lime slice.

Malibu Pot O' Gold

½ oz. Malibu pineapple rum
½ oz. Malibu rum
1 oz. pineapple juice
Shamrock or parsley for garnish

Shake and serve straight up in a martini glass. Garnish with a lucky shamrock or parsley.

Malibu Rain

1 oz. Finlandia vodka
½ oz. Malibu coconut rum
Splash orange juice

Serve over ice in a Collins glass.

Malibu Shake

1½ oz. Malibu coconut rum
1 oz. white crème de menthe
3 oz. pineapple juice
2 oz. cream

Blend with ice until smooth.

Mango Breeze

1 oz. Alizé wild passion liqueur
1 oz. vodka
1 oz. mango juice

Blend, and serve over ice in a rocks glass.

Mango Brulée

1½ oz. Malibu mango rum
1½ oz. Hiram Walker mango schnapps
1 oz. orange juice
1 oz. light cream
Mango or orange slice for garnish

Shake and strain into a martini glass. Garnish
with a mango or orange slice.

Mango Green Tea Frappé

1 oz. Stolichnaya vodka, light rum, or pre-
    mium tequila
2 oz. Hiram Walker mango schnapps
¾ oz. Monin green tea syrup
1¼ oz. sweet and sour mix (Dissolve 1 tsp.
    sugar in 3 oz. water. Add 2 oz. lemon juice.)
2 lemon squeezes
Lemon corkscrew for garnish
Mint sprig for garnish

Blend the first five ingredients with 1 cup ice
until smooth. Pour into a glass, and garnish
with the lemon corkscrew and mint sprig.

Mango Mama

1 oz. Southern Comfort
1 oz. Hiram Walker mango schnapps
2 oz. orange juice

Shake with ice, and serve over ice.

Mangorita

Salt to rim glass
1½ oz. tequila
1 oz. Hiram Walker mango schnapps
¼ oz. Hiram Walker triple sec
½ oz. lime juice

Rim a margarita glass with salt. Shake or blend
liquids with ice, and pour into the margarita
glass.

Mango Splash

1½ oz. rum
1 oz. Hiram Walker mango schnapps
2 oz. lemon-lime sour mix (Dissolve 1 tsp.
    sugar in 3 oz. water. Add 2 oz. lemon juice.)
2 oz. club soda
Lemon wedge for garnish

Serve liquids in a tall glass over ice. Garnish
with the lemon wedge.

Mango Surprise

¼ oz. Captain Morgan original spiced rum
½ oz. pineapple juice
½ oz. sweet and sour mix (Dissolve 1 tsp.
    sugar in 3 oz. water. Add 2 oz. lemon juice.)
¼ oz. grenadine
Pineapple slice for garnish

Shake with ice and strain into a highball glass.
Garnish with the pineapple slice.

Mango Tango

1½ oz. premium tequila
1 oz. Hiram Walker mango schnapps
½ oz. Hiram Walker triple sec
3–4 oz. pineapple juice

Serve over ice in a rocks glass.

Manhattan East

1 oz. Canton melon liqueur
1½ oz. bourbon
½ oz. dry sake
2 dashes Peychaud's bitters
Orange peel for garnish

Serve in a chilled martini glass, and garnish with the orange peel.

Margarita Madres

1¼ oz. José Cuervo Especial tequila
½ oz. Cointreau
1½ oz. sweet and sour mix (Dissolve 1 tsp. sugar in 3 oz. water. Add 2 oz. lemon juice.)
1½ oz. orange juice
1½ oz. cranberry juice
Lime slice for garnish

Blend with crushed ice and garnish with the lime slice.

Martini & Rossi Prosecco Bellini

2 oz. white peach purée
Squeeze fresh lemon
Martini & Rossi Prosecco to top, chilled

Pour the first two ingredients into a champagne glass. Top with the Prosecco.

Mediterranean Caipirinha

3 strawberries, chopped
3 grapes, chopped
4 fresh basil leaves
1 tsp. sugar
2 oz. Sagatiba pura cachaça

Muddle fruit with sugar and basil in a cocktail shaker until the sugar is dissolved in the juice. Add the cachaça and ice, and shake well. Serve in an old-fashioned glass.

Melon Baller

¼ cup cubed fresh watermelon
¾ oz. simple syrup (Dissolve 1 part sugar in 1 part boiling water. Let cool.)
2 oz. Remy Martin VSOP

Muddle, and strain the watermelon. Add the watermelon juice and simple syrup to a cocktail shaker. Add the brandy and ice. Shake well, and strain into a martini glass.

Melon Colada

1 oz. Hiram Walker melon liqueur
1 oz. Malibu coconut rum
1 oz. pineapple juice
1 oz. piña colada mix

Blend with crushed ice.

Miami Ice

1 oz. José Cuervo Tradicional tequila
½ oz. Smirnoff vodka
½ oz. light rum
2 oz. pineapple juice
1 oz. orange juice
½ oz. Coco Lopez cream of coconut

Shake with crushed ice and pour into a glass over crushed ice.

Minuteman

1½ oz. Laird's AppleJack
4 oz. apple cider
3 dashes Angostura bitters
Lemon wedge for garnish

Pour liquids into a tall glass over ice. Stir well to incorporate bitters. Garnish with the lemon wedge.

Mojito Tecate Light

Sugar to rim glass
6 mint leaves
4 tbsp. sugar syrup
2 tbsp. lemon juice
2 tbsp. white rum
12 oz. cold Tecate Light

Rim a tall glass with sugar. Crush the mint leaves in with the glass. Add the remaining ingredients, shake, and enjoy!

Monkey Business

1 oz. Finlandia cranberry fusion vodka
¼ oz. Malibu coconut rum
1 oz. pineapple juice

Shake with ice. Serve over ice.

Moonstruck in Malibu

Crushed candy hearts to rim glass
1 oz. Malibu passion fruit rum
1 oz. Malibu pineapple rum
1½ oz. pomegranate juice
4 oz. G. H. Mumm champagne

Rim a champagne flute with the candy hearts. Stir
liquids together and serve in champagne flute.

Myer's Jump Up and Kiss Me

1¼ oz. Myer's original dark rum
4 oz. pineapple juice
½ oz. fresh lime juice
Dash bitters
Pineapple stick for garnish
Lime slice for garnish

Combine liquids, and pour into a glass over ice.
Garnish with a pineapple stick and lime slice.

Myrtle Bank Punch

1¼ oz. Captain Morgan original spiced rum
¼ oz. grenadine
1 oz. fresh lime juice
1 tsp. sugar
¼ oz. cherry liqueur
Orange wedge or fruit flag for garnish

Pour the first four ingredients into a glass over crushed ice. Top with the cherry liqueur, and garnish with a fruit flag or orange wedge.

Naked Berry

2 oz. Stolichnaya blakberi vodka
1 oz. Hiram Walker white peach schnapps
2 oz. sweet and sour mix (Dissolve 1 tsp. sugar in 3 oz. water. Add 2 oz. lemon juice.)
1 oz. cola
Squeeze lemon juice for garnish

Shake the first three ingredients vigorously with ice. Strain into a glass over ice. Top with cola, and garnish with a squeeze of lemon juice.

Naked Lemon Drop

½ Stolichnaya ohranj vodka
½ oz. Hiram Walker white peach schnapps
Squeeze lemon juice

Shake vigorously with ice. Strain into a chilled shot or rocks glass.

Naked Navel

2 oz. Stolichnaya vodka
1 oz. Hiram Walker white peach schnapps
2 oz. orange juice

Build in a highball glass over ice. Use 100-proof vodka for a Pierced Navel, and agave tequila for a Barbed Navel.

Naked Russian

2 oz. Stolichnaya blakberi vodka
1 oz. Hiram Walker white peach schnapps
2 oz. fresh lemon juice
1 oz. simple syrup (Dissolve 1 part sugar in 1
    part boiling water. Let cool.)
2 blackberries for garnish

Shake with ice, and strain into a chilled martini glass. Garnish with two blackberries on a cocktail stick.

Natural Mojito

Sugar to rim glass
3 oz. Korbel natural champagne
1 oz. Appleton Estate Jamaican rum
2 oz. soda
Mint sprig for garnish
Sugarcane for garnish

Rim the glass with sugar. Pour liquids into the glass over ice. Garnish with the mint sprig and sugarcane.

Natural Sparkler

Korbel natural champagne to fill
1 oz. strawberry purée
Chocolate-covered strawberries for garnish

Serve in a champagne glass, and garnish with
the chocolate-covered strawberries.

Neon

1 oz. Black Haus schnapps
½ oz. Captain Morgan Parrot Bay coconut rum
3 oz. pineapple juice

Serve on the rocks.

New Orleans Day

2 oz. Coco Lopez cream of coconut
1 oz. butterscotch schnapps
1 oz. half-and-half

Blend with 1 cup ice until smooth.

Orange Mojo'Rita Cocktail

1 orange, cut into wedges, plus extra for garnish
1 cup fresh mint leaves
3 cups José Cuervo golden margarita mix
1 cup José Cuervo Especial tequila
Mint sprig for garnish
Splash crème de menthe

Place the oranges, mint leaves, mix, and tequila in a pitcher, and muddle until the flavors distribute and the orange and mint start to break down. Strain the mixture into a large Collins glass over crushed ice, orange wedges, and mint leaves. Top with the splash of crème de menthe. Garnish with the mint and orange wedges, and serve.

Orange Sorbet Lopez

2 oz. Coco Lopez cream of coconut
1 oz. orange juice
1 scoop orange sherbet

Blend with 1 cup ice until smooth.

Original Bahama Mama

2 parts spiced rum
2 parts Stirrings piña colada mix
1 part coffee liqueur
Wedge pineapple for garnish

Blend with 2 cups ice until creamy. Serve in a daiquiri glass. Garnish with the pineapple wedge.

Original Sex on the Beach

1 oz. Midori melon liqueur
1 oz. vodka
1 oz. raspberry liqueur
2 oz. pineapple juice
2 oz. cranberry juice

Shake and serve on the rocks or strain into a chilled martini glass.

Paradise Punch

1 oz. Tommy Bahama golden sun rum
1 oz. pineapple juice
Splash orange juice
Orange wedge for garnish

Shake liquids with ice. Pour into a rocks glass, and garnish with the orange wedge.

Passion and Cream

Cinnamon sugar to rim glass
3 oz. Stolichnaya vanil vodka
2 oz. Hiram Walker blueberry passion
    schnapps
2 oz. Hiram Walker white peach schnapps
4 oz. half-and-half
Peach slice for garnish

Rim a martini glass with cinnamon sugar. Shake liquids vigorously with ice. Strain into the martini glass. Garnish with the peach slice.

Passion and Pagne

3 oz. Alizé red passion
3 oz. Taittinger champagne

Serve chilled in a champagne flute.

Passion Fruit Cosmo

1¼ oz. Smirnoff passion fruit-flavored vodka
¼ oz. triple sec
Splash fresh lime juice
Splash cranberry juice
Lime slice for garnish

Shake liquids with ice. Strain into a martini glass. Garnish with the lime slice.

Passion Fruit Mai Tai

1¼ oz. Smirnoff passion fruit-flavored vodka
¼ oz. almond liqueur
¾ oz. fresh lime juice
¼ oz. grenadine
Orange slice for garnish
Maraschino cherry for garnish

Build in a Collins glass over ice, and garnish with the orange slice and cherry.

Passion Fruit Mimosa

1 tbsp. Grand Marnier
3 tbsp. passion-fruit juice
4 oz. Korbel champagne
Orange peel twist for garnish

Combine the first two ingredients in a glass, and top with the champagne. Garnish with the orange peel twist.

Passion Fruit Punch

1½ oz. Smirnoff passion fruit-flavored vodka
Splash cranberry juice
Splash pineapple juice
Splash grapefruit juice
2 dashes bitters
Lemon-lime soda to top
Pineapple wedge for garnish
Orange slice for garnish
Maraschino cherry for garnish

Build liquids in a Collins glass over ice, and garnish with the fruit.

Passion Lemonade

1½ oz. Smirnoff passion fruit-flavored vodka
2 oz. lemonade
Lemon wedge for garnish

Serve in a tall glass on the rocks, and garnish with the lemon wedge.

Passionate Summer Fling

2 oz. SKYY Infusions passion fruit vodka
½ oz. peach schnapps
2 oz. orange juice
1 oz. fresh lemon juice
1 oz. simple syrup (Dissolve 1 part sugar in 1
    part boiling water. Let cool.)
Peach slice for garnish

Shake liquids vigorously with ice. Strain into a
rocks glass. Garnish with the peach slice.

Passionpolitan

1 oz. Captain Morgan Parrot Bay passion fruit
    rum
¼ oz. triple sec
2 oz. cranberry juice
Squeeze lime juice
Lime wedge for garnish

Pour into a glass over ice, and stir. Garnish
with the lime wedge.

PB Breeze

1½ oz. Captain Morgan Parrot Bay coconut
    rum
2 oz. cranberry juice
2 oz. pineapple juice
Pineapple slice for garnish

Pour liquids into a glass over ice, and stir.
Garnish with the pineapple slice.

Peaches & Cream

1½ oz. DeKuyper peachtree schnapps
1½ oz. half-and-half or milk

Shake and serve over ice in a rocks glass.

Peaches & Cream Extreme

2 oz. Stolichnaya vanil vodka
2 oz. Hiram Walker white peach schnapps
1 oz. Hiram Walker white crème de cacao
2 oz. half-and-half
1 oz. cola to top

Shake vigorously with ice. Strain into a high-ball glass over ice, and top with cola.

Peach Margarita

¾ oz. Sauza blanco tequila
¾ oz. DeKuyper peachtree schnapps
1½ oz. sweet and sour mix (Dissolve 1 tsp. sugar in 3 oz. water. Add 2 oz. lemon juice.)

Shake with ice. Serve on the rocks or in a chilled martini glass.

Peachsicle

1½ oz. DeKuyper peachtree schnapps
Orange juice to fill

Shake with ice and serve in a tall glass.

Peach Snap

2 thin slices fresh ginger, muddled
5 oz. Stolichnaya ohranj vodka
3 oz. Hiram Walker white peach schnapps
4 oz. sweet and sour mix (Dissolve 1 tsp.
   sugar in 3 oz. water. Add 2 oz. lemon
   juice.)
Candied ginger slice for garnish

Shake vigorously with ice. Strain into martini glass. Garnish with the ginger slice, and serve.

Peachtree Daiquiri

2 oz. DeKuyper peachtree schnapps
1 oz. Bacardi rum
4 oz. sweet and sour mix (Dissolve 1 tsp.
   sugar in 3 oz. water. Add 2 oz. lemon
   juice.)

Blend with ½ cup crushed ice, and serve in an 8-oz. glass.

Peachtree Margarita

2 oz. DeKuyper peachtree schnapps
1 oz. Sauza silver tequila
4 oz. sweet and sour mix (Dissolve 1 tsp. sugar
   in 3 oz. water. Add 2 oz. lemon juice.)
½ cup crushed ice

Blend with the ice, and serve in a large glass.

Pear

2 oz. 1800 tequila
½ oz. limoncello
½ oz. pear purée
½ oz. white cranberry juice
Lime wheel or pear slice for garnish

Shake liquids with ice. Strain into a martini glass. Garnish with the lime wheel or pear slice.

Pear Tart

1 oz. Stolichnaya citros vodka
1 oz. Hiram Walker pear schnapps
1 oz. fresh lemon juice
Lemon peel for garnish

Shake and strain into a martini glass. Garnish with the lemon peel.

Perfumed Pomegranate

20 fresh pomegranate seeds
½ oz. simple syrup (Dissolve 1 part sugar in 1
    part boiling water. Let cool.)
1 oz. Belvedere vodka
½ oz. rose tea syrup
Dash rose petal liqueur
Dash lemon juice
Moët et Chandon brut imperial champagne
    to top
Rose petal for garnish

Muddle the pomegranate with the simple
syrup, add the next four ingredients, and shake
with cubed ice. Strain using a fine strainer into
a chilled champagne flute, and top with the
champagne. Garnish with the rose petal.

Piña Koalapear

2 oz. DeKuyper harvest pear schnapps
1 oz. CocoRibe coconut rum
1 oz. cream
Pineapple slice for garnish
Maraschino cherry for garnish

Blend liquids with ice. Garnish with the pineapple slice and cherry.

Pineapple & Kaffir Leaf Collins

2-3 fresh kaffir lime leaves plus an extra for
    garnish
½ oz. simple syrup (Dissolve 1 part sugar in 1
    part boiling water. Let cool.)
2 oz. Belvedere cytrus vodka
¾ oz. fresh lime juice
2 oz. fresh pineapple juice

Tear leaves, and place into a highball glass.
Add the simple syrup, and press lightly to
release the oils. Add the next two ingredients,
and top with crushed ice. Churn. Top with the
pineapple juice and re-top with crushed ice.
Garnish with two straws and a kaffir lime leaf.

Pineapple-Orange Margarita

1½ oz. José Cuervo Especial tequila
2 oz. José Cuervo margarita mix, classic lime
    flavor
1 oz. pineapple juice
1 oz. orange juice
1 tbsp. sugar
Pineapple spears and Maraschino cherries for
    garnish

Mix in a cocktail shaker with a spoon, and
strain into a rocks glass over ice. Garnish with
the pineapple spears and cherries.

Pink Cadillac

1 oz. Stolichnaya vanil vodka
1 oz. Hiram Walker pink grapefruit schnapps
2 oz. cranberry juice
1 oz. pineapple juice
Fresh raspberry for garnish

Serve in a tall glass over ice. Garnish with the
fresh raspberry.

Pink Lemonade

1¼ oz. Captain Morgan original spiced rum
3 oz. cranberry juice
2 oz. club soda
¼ oz. fresh lemon juice
Orange slice for garnish

Build in a glass over ice. Garnish with the
orange slice.

Pink Panther

1¼ oz. Bacardi rum
¾ oz. fresh lemon juice
¾ oz. cream
½ oz. Major Peters' grenadine

Mix in a shaker or blender with ice, and strain
into a cocktail glass.

Pink Slip

1 oz. Stolichnaya razberri vodka
1 oz. Hiram Walker pink grapefruit schnapps
4 oz. cranberry juice
Grapefruit chunk for garnish

Build in a glass over ice. Garnish with the grapefruit chunk.

Pinktini

1 oz. Stolichnaya vodka
1 oz. Hiram Walker pink grapefruit schnapps
Lemon wedge for garnish

Shake and strain into a martini glass. Garnish with the lemon wedge.

Pit Bull

1 oz. SKYY Infusions cherry vodka
1 oz. Red Bull

Serve as a shot or on the rocks.

Poma-Mama-Bu

1½ oz. Malibu tropical banana rum
1½ oz. Hiram Walker pomegranate schnapps
3–5 oz. orange-pineapple juice mix
Fruit of your choice for garnish

Serve in a tall glass over ice, and garnish with
the fruit.

Pomegranate

Sugar to rim glass
2 oz. 1800 tequila
1 oz. PAMA pomegranate liqueur
½ oz. pineapple juice

Rim a martini glass with sugar. Shake liquids
with ice. Strain into the martini glass.

Pomegranate Margarita Martini

2 cups José Cuervo golden margarita mix
¼ cup pomegranate juice
¼ cup José Cuervo Especial tequila
Juice 1 lime
Lime zest curl for garnish

Shake liquids vigorously with ice. Strain into a
chilled martini glass, and garnish with the lime
zest curl.

POMMarvelous

4 oz. champagne
½ oz. POM Wonderful pomegranate juice
½ oz. Cointreau
Fresh pomegranate seeds for garnish
Orange twist for garnish

Pour into a glass, and serve straight up or
on the rocks. Garnish with the pomegranate
seeds and orange twist.

Pom Passion Shot

1 oz. Stolichnaya citros vodka
1 oz. Hiram Walker blueberry passion
    schnapps
1 oz. Hiram Walker pomegranate schnapps
1 oz. sweet and sour mix (Dissolve 1 tsp.
    sugar in 3 oz. water. Add 2 oz. lemon
    juice.)

Shake vigorously with ice. Strain into a chilled
shot or rocks glass.

Pompered Princess

2 oz. Hiram Walker pomegranate schnapps
3 oz. champagne
Strawberry for garnish

Stir liquids gently. Garnish with the strawberry.

Posmo

1½ oz. Hiram Walker pomegranate schnapps
1½ oz. Stolichnaya citros vodka
¼ oz. Hiram Walker triple sec
1 oz. cranberry juice
½ oz. fresh lime juice
Lime wedge for garnish

Shake and strain into a martini glass. Garnish with the lime wedge.

Pretty in Purple

2 oz. SKYY vodka
1½ oz. pomegranate juice
½ oz. blue curaçao
Orange slice for garnish

Shake liquids with ice. Pour into a chilled martini glass, and garnish with the orange slice.

Purple Pants

1½ oz. SKYY Infusions grape vodka
½ oz. blue curaçao
½ oz. sloe gin

Shake with ice, and serve as a shot on the rocks.

Author's Note: The next few recipes contain Purple, a new antioxidant beverage. You can find it at GNC stores. I hope you try and enjoy!

Purple People Eater

1½ oz. SKYY Infusions grape vodka
½ oz. Purple antioxidant drink
½ oz. chilled champagne

Serve as a shot or in a tall glass without ice.

Purple Rita

Salt to rim glass
1 oz. Purple antioxidant drink
1 oz. tequila
1 oz. Cointreau
Fresh lime juice to taste
Simple syrup (Dissolve 1 part sugar in 1 part
    boiling water. Let cool.)

Rim a martini glass with salt. Shake liquids with ice and strain. Serve in the martini glass.

Purple Slush

1 oz. Purple antioxidant drink
1½ oz. rum
½ oz. fresh lemon juice
½ oz. simple syrup (Dissolve 1 part sugar in 1
    part boiling water. Let cool.)
Mint sprig for garnish

Shake well with ice and serve over crushed ice.
Garnish with a mint sprig.

Purple Sweetheart

1 oz. Purple antioxidant drink
1½ oz. Sobieski vodka
1 oz. Cointreau
Fresh lime to taste
Lemon rind shoelace for garnish

Shake liquids vigorously with ice. Strain into
a frozen martini glass. Garnish with the lemon
rind shoelace.

Raspberry Delight

¾ oz. Drambuie
¾ oz. Chambord
½ oz. DeKuyper coffee liqueur
1 scoop vanilla ice cream
6 fresh raspberries

Blend with crushed ice.

Raspberry Green Tea Frappé

1 oz. Stolichnaya vodka
2 oz. Hiram Walker raspberry schnapps
¾ oz. Monin green tea syrup
1¼ oz. sweet and sour mix (Dissolve 1 tsp.
    sugar in 3 oz. water. Add 2 oz. lemon juice.)
2 lemon squeezes
3 frozen raspberries for garnish
Mint sprig for garnish

Blend with 1 cup ice until smooth. Pour into a glass and garnish with the 3 raspberries and the mint sprig.

Raw Diamond

Salt to rim glass
1 oz. 1800 select silver tequila
¼ oz. pear purée
¼ oz. fresh lime juice
¼ oz. agave nectar
Splash Chambord or blue curaçao

Lightly rim a highball glass with salt. Shake the first four ingredients vigorously with ice. Pour into salt-rimmed glass. Float Chambord or curaçao for a drizzle effect.

Red Apple

1½ oz. Laird's AppleJack
3 oz. Red Bull
1 oz. cranberry juice

Pour into a tall glass over ice.

Red Passion

1½ oz. Smirnoff passion fruit-flavored vodka
3 oz. cranberry juice
Lemon-lime twist for garnish

Build in a rocks glass, and garnish with a lemon-lime twist.

Red Snapper

1 oz. Crown Royal Special Reserve
¼ oz. amaretto
5 oz. cranberry juice

Pour into a highball glass over ice, and stir.

Remy Knockout

1½ oz. Remy Martin VSOP
1 oz. Cointreau
Splash pineapple juice
Splash cranberry juice

Shake liquids with ice. Serve on the rocks. or strain into a chilled martini glass.

Remy Sidecar

Sugar to rim glass
1½ oz. Remy Martin VSOP
½ oz. Cointreau
½ tsp. fresh lemon juice

Rim a martini glass with sugar, and chill. Shake liquids vigorously with ice. Strain into a chilled martini glass.

Remy Stinger

1¾ oz. Remy Martin VSOP
¼ oz. white crème de menthe

Shake well with ice. Strain into a chilled martini glass.

Remy Viper

1½ oz. Remy Martin VSOP
3 oz. Piper-Heidsieck brut champagne

Pour the brandy into a champagne glass, and top with the champagne.

Rhum Barbancourt Freeze

2 oz. Rhum Barbancourt
1 oz. triple sec
1 oz. grapefruit juice
2 oz. orange juice
½ oz. fresh lime juice
Orange wedge for garnish

Blend liquids with ⅓ cup ice cubes until smooth, about 30 seconds. Pour into a glass, and garnish with the orange wedge.

Rosarita Margarita

1½ oz. José Cuervo Especial tequila
3 oz. José Cuervo margarita mix, classic lime
   flavor
1 oz. cranberry juice
1 cup crushed ice
Handful cranberries (frozen or fresh)

Blend. Pour entire contents into a margarita glass. Note: The cranberries should fleck throughout the drink.

Royal Tropic

½ oz. Crown Royal Special Reserve
½ oz. almond liqueur
½ oz. raspberry liqueur
2 oz. cranberry juice
2 oz. pineapple juice

Pour into a rocks glass over ice, and stir.

Rude Cosmopolitan

1 oz. José Cuervo Clásico tequila
1.5 oz. Grand Marnier
1 oz. cranberry juice
Juice of 1 lime
Lime wedge for garnish

Shake liquids over ice. Serve in a chilled martini glass. Garnish with the lime wedge.

Rum Runner

¾ oz. Captain Morgan original spiced rum
¼ oz. blackberry liqueur
¼ oz. crème de bananes
2 oz. orange juice
½ oz. grenadine
8 oz. crushed ice
Orange slice for garnish

Blend liquids and ice until smooth. Serve in a cocktail glass, and garnish with the orange slice.

Rum Yum

1 oz. Baileys Irish cream
1 oz. Malibu rum
1 oz. cream or milk

Blend with ice.

Saga Summer

1½ oz. Sagatiba pura cachaça
¾ oz. orange liqueur or Cointreau
2 slices cucumber plus extra for garnish
2 oz. cranberry juice
2 oz. sliced lemon, lime, orange, and berries
    or seasonal fruits
Ginger ale to top

Shake the first five ingredients with ice. Pour
into a large fluted glass, top with ginger ale,
and garnish with the cucumber slice.

Sagatiba Classic Caipirinha

½ lime cut in wedges
2 tsp. sugar
2 oz. Sagatiba pura cachaça

Muddle the lime and sugar. Add ice, pour in
the liquor, and shake well.

Saint

4 lime wedges
5 large mint leaves
½ oz. agave nectar
2 oz. 1800 tequila
½ oz. St. Germain elderflower liqueur
Splash club soda

Muddle the lime, mint, and nectar in the bottom of a glass. Top with ice, add liquids, shake, and pour all contents into a glass to serve. Top with the club soda.

Sara's Flavor Rush

1 oz. Sauza blanco tequila
3 oz. ginger ale
Squeeze lime wedge

Serve in a tall glass over ice.

Sauza Gold Berri-tini

¾ oz. Sauza gold tequila
¾ oz. Razzmatazz
1 ½ oz. sweet and sour mix (Dissolve 1 tsp. sugar in 3 oz. water. Add 2 oz. lemon juice.)

Shake with ice and serve over ice or in a chilled martini glass.

Sauza Gold Mexitini

1 oz. DeKuyper pucker apple
1 oz. Sauza gold tequila
¾ oz. pineapple juice

Shake with ice. Serve over ice or in a chilled
martini glass.

Sauza Gold Nectar

2 oz. Sauza gold tequila
½ oz. DeKuyper peachtree schnapps

Shake with ice. Serve over ice or in a chilled
martini glass.

Scarlett Kiss

2 oz. Drambuie
3 oz. cranberry juice

Serve in a tall glass over ice.

Scotch Smoothie

1 oz. Coco Lopez cream of coconut
1¼ oz. scotch
½ oz. Baileys Irish cream
½ oz. almond liqueur
2 scoops vanilla ice cream

Blend with crushed ice.

Scottish Iced Tea

2 oz. Drambuie
3 oz. freshly brewed unsweetened iced tea
Lemon slice or mint sprig for garnish

Serve in a tall glass, and garnish with the lemon slice or mint sprig.

Select Silver Dog

Salt to rim glass
1½ oz. 1800 tequila
3 oz. grapefruit juice
Lime wedge for garnish

Rim a martini glass with salt. Combine liquids with crushed ice, and pour into the glass filled with ice. Garnish with the lime wedge.

Sex A' Peel

½ banana
1¼ oz. simple syrup (Dissolve 1 part sugar in 1 part boiling water. Let cool.)
Splash balsamic vinegar
2 oz. Remy Martin VSOP
Lemon peel for garnish

Muddle and strain the banana. Add juice from the banana with the simple syrup and balsamic vinegar in a cocktail shaker. Add the brandy and ice. Shake well, and strain into a martini glass. Garnish with a lemon twist.

Shaman

1½ oz. Smirnoff blueberry-flavored vodka
1 oz. açai juice
½ oz. agave nectar
½ oz. Key lime juice
Key lime wheel for garnish

Shake liquids and serve in a martini glass garnished with the Key lime wheel.

Silver White Grape Sour

1½ oz. Smirnoff white grape vodka
¾ oz. fresh lemon juice
¾ oz. simple syrup (Dissolve 1 part sugar in 1 part boiling water. Let cool.)
Bar spoon pomegranate molasses
Small bunch champagne grapes for garnish

Shake liquids briefly with ice. Strain into a frosted martini glass. Garnish with a small bunch of champagne grapes.

SKYY Cherry Cheesecake

1½ oz. SKYY Infusions cherry vodka
½ oz. cranberry juice
½ oz. simple syrup (Dissolve 1 part sugar in 1
    part boiling water. Let cool.)
½ oz. amaretto
Dollop whipped cream for garnish
Maraschino cherry for garnish

Shake liquids. Serve on the rocks with the dollop of whipped cream and the cherry.

SKYY Citroni

2 oz. SKYY Infusions citrus vodka
Splash Cinzano vermouth
Orange slice for garnish

Stir with ice. Serve in a chilled martini glass and float the orange slice.

SKYY Infusions Cherry and Rye

1½ oz. SKYY Infusions cherry vodka
1 oz. fresh lemon juice
½ oz. Cointreau
½ oz. sweet vermouth
¾ oz. rye whiskey
2 oz. soda
Lemon zest for garnish
Maraschino cherry for garnish

Shake liquids vigorously with ice. Strain into a
tall pilsner-style glass. Garnish with the lemon
zest and cherry.

SKYY Infusions Cherry Coke

4 oz. SKYY Infusions cherry vodka
2 oz. Carpano Punt e Mes vermouth
1 oz. fresh lemon juice
1 oz. simple syrup (Dissolve 1 part sugar in 1
    part boiling water. Let cool.)
Fresh cherries on a pick for garnish

Shake liquids vigorously with ice. Strain into
a rocks glass. Garnish with the fresh cherries
on a pick.

SKYY Infusions Grape Ginger Swizzle

4 blackberries plus extra for garnish
4 slices fresh ginger, peeled
1 tsp. raw sugar
1½ oz. SKYY Infusions grape vodka
Ginger ale to top
Candied ginger for garnish

Muddle the fresh blackberries, ginger, and sugar in a pint glass. Add ice and the vodka. Shake vigorously, and strain into a Collins glass over fresh ice. Top with the ginger ale, and garnish with the blackberries and candied ginger.

SKYY Infusions Passion Fruit Maracuja Melange

2 oz. SKYY Infusions passion fruit vodka
½ oz. peach schnapps
2 oz. orange juice
1 oz. fresh lemon juice
1 oz. simple syrup (Dissolve 1 part sugar in 1
    part boiling water. Let cool.)
Peach slice for garnish

Shake liquids vigorously with ice. Strain into a rocks glass. Garnish with the peach slice.

SKYY Infusions Passion Paradox Tea

1½ oz. SKYY Infusions passion fruit vodka
¾ oz. simple syrup (Dissolve 1 part sugar in 1 part boiling water. Let cool.)
4 oz. brewed Republic of Tea mango Ceylon black tea
Dried mango for garnish

Build in a tall glass, and garnish with the dried mango.

SKYY Infusions Perbacco

2 oz. SKYY Infusions grape vodka
1 oz. Lillet Blanc apéritif wine
2 oz. pineapple juice
1 oz. fresh lime juice
1 oz. simple syrup (Dissolve 1 part sugar in 1 part boiling water. Let cool.)
Fresh grapes on a toothpick for garnish

Shake liquids vigorously with ice. Strain into a stemless champagne flute. Garnish with the grapes on a toothpick.

SKYY Infusions Raspberry Plum Fun

2 oz. SKYY Infusions raspberry vodka
4 fresh raspberries plus 1 for garnish
1 oz. black plum purée
3 fresh lime wedges
¼ oz. simple syrup (Dissolve 1 part sugar in 1
    part boiling water. Let cool.)
Lime slice for garnish

Muddle fresh raspberries, plum purée, lime wedges, and simple syrup in a pint glass with ice. Add the vodka, and shake vigorously. Strain into a coupe glass. Garnish with the lime slice and raspberry.

SKYY Infusions Rosemary Lemon Fizz

½ organic rosemary sprig plus extra for garnish
½ oz. Meyer lemon juice
½ oz. simple syrup (Dissolve 1 part sugar in 1
    part boiling water. Let cool.)
1½ oz. SKYY Infusions citrus vodka
Dash club soda

Muddle the rosemary with the lemon juice and simple syrup in a shaker. Add ice and the vodka, and shake. Strain over fresh ice into a rocks glass, and top with the soda. Garnish with the fresh rosemary sprig.

SKYY Infusions Vanilla Citrus Tea

1½ oz. SKYY Infusions citrus vodka
½ oz. simple syrup (Dissolve 1 part sugar in 1
    part boiling water. Let cool.)
4 oz. Republic of Tea vanilla almond black tea
Lemon slice for garnish

Build in a Collins glass, and garnish with the lemon slice.

SKYY Scraper

1½ oz. SKYY Infusions citrus vodka
½ oz. cranberry juice
½ oz. pineapple juice

Serve in a tall glass over ice.

SKYY Stinger

Sugar to rim glass
2 oz. SKYY Infusions citrus vodka
¼ oz. white crème de menthe

Rim a martini glass with sugar. Shake liquids with ice. Strain into the martini glass.

Slammer

1 oz. tequila
3 oz. Korbel chardonnay champagne

Pour the tequila into an oversized shot glass.
Add the champagne, and slam the glass onto
the bar counter or table. Serve immediately.

Slippery Banana

½ oz. Malibu coconut rum
½ oz. Malibu tropical banana rum
½ oz. pineapple juice
Dash Maraschino cherry juice

Shake with ice, and serve on the rocks in a
chilled martini glass.

Smirnoff Watermelon Martini

1 oz. Smirnoff watermelon vodka
Splash sweet and sour mix (Dissolve 1 tsp.
    sugar in 3 oz. water. Add 2 oz. lemon
    juice.)
Splash cranberry juice
Fresh watermelon wedge for garnish

Shake liquids and strain into a martini glass.
Garnish with the fresh watermelon wedge.

Smirnoff White Grape on the Beach

1 oz. Smirnoff white grape vodka
¼ oz. peach schnapps
¼ oz. triple sec
Splash cranberry juice
Splash sweet and sour mix (Dissolve 1 tsp.
    sugar in 3 oz. water. Add 2 oz. lemon
    juice.)
Maraschino cherry for garnish

Shake liquids with ice. Strain into a martini
glass. Garnish with the cherry.

Soulmate

4 oz. Korbel brut champagne
1 oz. raspberry liqueur or Chambord
Splash cranberry juice

Stir in a large champagne flute, and serve
immediately.

South Peach

6 oz. Korbel brut or extra dry champagne
Splash peach schnapps
Splash cranberry juice or cranberry-juice drink

Pour champagne into a large champagne flute,
and slowly stir in the schnapps and cranberry
juice.

Southern Orleans

1 oz. Southern Comfort
⅔ oz. sweet and sour mix (Dissolve 1 tsp.
    sugar in 3 oz. water. Add 2 oz. lemon
    juice.)
⅔ oz. chilled Korbel brut champagne
1 sugar cube
¼ oz. grenadine
Lime wheel for garnish

Shake the first three ingredients vigorously.
Strain into a cocktail glass over the sugar
cube. Add the grenadine on top but do not stir.
Garnish with the lime wheel.

Sparkling Margarita

Splash Cointreau plus extra to rim glass
Sugar to rim glass
Splash lime juice
Splash orange juice
Lime twist for garnish

Rim a frosted martini glass with Cointreau and
sugar. Pour liquids into the glass. Garnish with
the lime twist.

Star-Spangled Swizzle

2 oz. Jim Beam black bourbon
1 oz. DeKuyper triple sec
½ oz. orange juice
½ oz. fresh lemon juice
½ oz. fresh lime juice

½ oz. pineapple juice
Splash DeKuyper blue curaçao
Splash sloe gin
Grated nutmeg for garnish
Maraschino cherry for garnish

Pour the first seven ingredients into a glass over ice. Top with a splash of the sloe gin. Garnish with the grated nutmeg and the cherry.

Strawberry Ginger Martini

2 oz. Canton melon liqueur
1 oz. gin or vodka
3 medium or 2 large strawberries
Squeeze lime juice

Serve in a chilled martini glass.

St. Simons Island

2 oz. Stolichnaya vodka
1 oz. Hiram Walker white peach schnapps
1 oz. orange juice
Peach slice for garnish
Orange slice for garnish

Blend with crushed ice until smooth. Pour into a hurricane glass, and garnish with the peach slice and orange slice.

Summer Berry Mojito

Stirrings mojito rimmer to rim glass
1½ oz. rum
1 oz. Stirrings wild blueberry martini
1 oz. Stirrings mojito
8 fresh blackberries
Splash soda

Rim glass with Stirrings mojito rimmer. Shake
the next three ingredients well with the blackberries. Top with a splash of the soda and
serve on the rocks.

Sunbelt

1½ oz. Gordon's gin
Grapefruit juice to fill

Pour the gin into a highball glass over ice. Fill
with the grapefruit juice.

Sunny SKYY Sitron

2 oz. SKYY Infusions citrus vodka
3 oz. orange juice

Pour into a tall glass over ice.

Sunshine State

2 oz. Stolichnaya citros vodka
1 oz. Hiram Walker pink grapefruit schnapps
1 oz. Hiram Walker tangerine schnapps
2 oz. orange juice
2 oz. grapefruit juice
Mint sprig for garnish

Pour liquids into a tall glass over ice. Garnish with the mint sprig.

Sunstroke

1½ oz. Smirnoff vodka
3 oz. grapefruit juice
Splash triple sec

Pour into a tall glass over ice. Stir.

Swaying Skirt Martini

1½ oz. Smirnoff passion fruit vodka
1 oz. guava nectar juice
¾ oz. fresh lime juice
¾ oz. simple syrup (Dissolve 1 part sugar in 1 part boiling water. Let cool.)
Maraschino cherry for garnish

Shake liquids with ice. Strain into a martini glass. Garnish with the cherry.

Tall Blueberry Bull

1 oz. Stolichnaya razberi vodka
1 oz. Hiram Walker blueberry passion
   schnapps
5 oz. energy drink of your choice

Build in a 14-oz. glass over ice.

Tall Tropical Bull

1 oz. Malibu mango rum
1 oz. Hiram Walker white peach schnapps
5 oz. energy drink of your choice

Build in a 14-oz. glass over ice.

Tang-a-Cream

2 oz. Hiram Walker tangerine schnapps
2 oz. of your favorite ice cream

Blend, and serve in a tall glass.

Tang Tart

1 oz. Stolichnaya citros vodka
1 oz. Hiram Walker tangerine schnapps
1 oz. lemon juice
Lemon peel for garnish

Shake liquids. Strain into a chilled martini
glass. Garnish with the lemon peel.

Teeny Weeny Woo Woo

1½ oz. DeKuyper peachtree schnapps
1½ oz. Gilbey's vodka
Splash cranberry juice
Peach wheel for garnish

Serve over ice in a rocks glass. Stir and garnish
with the peach wheel.

Tequila Mockingbird

¾ oz. José Cuervo Tradicional tequila
¾ oz. Smirnoff vodka
2 oz. orange juice
1 oz. energy drink
Orange slice for garnish

Stir liquids well with ice in a glass. Serve in
a highball glass, and garnish with the orange
slice.

Three Wise Men

½ oz. José Cuervo Tradicional tequila
½ oz. Goldschläger schnapps
½ oz. Rumple Minze schnapps

Mix with ice, and strain into a shot glass.

Tidal Wave

1½ oz. Laird's AppleJack
4 oz. orange juice
Splash cranberry juice
Orange slice for garnish

Pour into a tall glass over ice. Garnish with the orange slice.

Topaz

2 oz. lychee tequila
¼ oz. white cranberry juice

Shake. Strain into a chilled martini glass.

Treasure

1¼ oz. Captain Morgan original spiced rum
¼ oz. Goldschläger schnapps

Chill, and serve in a shot glass.

Tropical Freeze Lopez

2 oz. Coco Lopez cream of coconut
1½ oz. orange juice
1½ oz. pineapple juice

Blend with 1 cup ice until smooth.

Tropicalia

2 oz. Sagatiba pura cachaça
1 oz. orange juice
1 oz. pineapple juice
1 oz. papaya juice
½ oz. simple syrup (Dissolve 1 part sugar in 1
    part boiling water. Let cool.)
½ oz. fresh lime juice
Orange wedge or star fruit slice for garnish

Shake liquids over ice. Strain into a martini
glass. Garnish with the orange wedge or star
fruit slice.

Tropical Passion

1 oz. Alizé red passion
1 oz. Midori melon liqueur
3 oz. pineapple juice
1 oz. orange juice
Pineapple wedge for garnish
Maraschino cherry for garnish

Blend liquids. Pour into a glass, and garnish with
the pineapple wedge and cherry on a spear.

Tropical Peachtree

1½ oz. DeKuyper peachtree schnapps
3 oz. orange-pineapple or orange-grapefruit
    juice
Splash club soda

Serve in a tall glass.

Tropical Splash

1½ oz. Captain Morgan Parrot Bay pineapple
    rum
5 oz. orange juice
Orange slice for garnish

Stir liquids well in a glass over ice. Garnish
with the orange slice.

Tropical Treasure

2½ oz. Captain Morgan Parrot Bay passion
    fruit rum
¼ oz. peach schnapps
2 oz. orange juice
Splash grenadine
2 oz. cream

Stir in a highball glass over ice.

Tropical Wave

1¼ oz. Captain Morgan original spiced rum
4 oz. orange juice
1 oz. cranberry juice
Pineapple slice for garnish

Shake liquids over ice. Pour into a tall glass.
Garnish with the pineapple slice.

Twist and Twirl

2 oz. SKYY vodka
½ oz. Dekuyper Raspberry Pucker
3 oz. cran-raspberry juice
Lime wedge for garnish

Mix liquids with crushed ice. Pour into a glass, and garnish with the lime wedge.

Twisted Island Breeze

2½ oz. Captain Morgan Parrot Bay pineapple rum
2 oz. grapefruit juice
Splash cranberry juice
2 oz. pineapple juice
Pineapple slice for garnish

Pour into a highball glass over ice, and stir. Garnish with the pineapple slice.

Vanilla

2 oz. 1800 tequila
1 oz. Frangelico
1 oz. Licor 43
½ oz. agave nectar

Shake with ice. Strain into a martini glass.

The Vixen

1½ oz. Smirnoff vodka
1 oz. pink grapefruit juice
1 oz. pink lemonade

Shake with ice, and serve in a chilled martini glass.

Wango Tango

2 oz. Malibu tropical banana rum
1½ oz. Hiram Walker tangerine schnapps
½ oz. lemon juice
4–5 oz. pineapple-orange juice mix
Fruit of your choice for garnish

Serve in a tall glass over ice. Garnish with the fruit.

Watermelon and Basil Martini

2 large chunks fresh watermelon plus extra
    for garnish
½ oz. simple syrup (Dissolve 1 part sugar in 1
    part boiling water. Let cool.)
2 oz. Belvedere vodka
2 basil leaves
¼ oz. fresh lemon juice

Muddle the 2 watermelon chunks with simple syrup in a shaker glass with ice. Add the remaining ingredients, and strain into a chilled martini glass. Garnish with the fresh watermelon chunk.

Watermelon Margarita

1 oz. DeKuyper pucker watermelon schnapps
2 oz. Sauza tequila
½ oz. DeKuyper signature triple sec
3 oz. sweet and sour mix (Dissolve 1 tsp. sugar
   in 3 oz. water. Add 2 oz. lemon juice.)

Blend with ice.

Wave Cutter

1½ oz. Bacardi rum
1 oz. cranberry juice
1 oz. orange juice
Maraschino cherry for garnish

Mix liquids over ice, and garnish with the
cherry.

White Cosmo

3 oz. vodka
1 oz. Cointreau
1 oz. white cranberry juice
Splash sweet and sour mix (Dissolve 1 tsp.
   sugar in 3 oz. water. Add 2 oz. lemon
   juice.)
Orange twist for garnish

Shake liquids with ice. Strain into a chilled
cocktail glass. Garnish with the orange twist.

White Grape Bamble

1¼ oz. Smirnoff white grape-flavored vodka
¾ oz. fresh lemon juice
¾ oz. simple syrup (Dissolve 1 part sugar in 1
    part boiling water. Let cool.)
¼ oz. blackberry liqueur
Lemon twist for garnish

Build the first three ingredients in a Collins
glass over ice. Float the blackberry liqueur,
and garnish with the lemon twist.

White Grape Champagne

¾ oz. Smirnoff white grape-flavored vodka
¾ oz. champagne
White grape for garnish

Serve in a champagne flute, and garnish with
the white grape.

White Grape Cosmo

1¼ oz. Smirnoff white grape-flavored vodka
¼ oz. triple sec
2 oz. cranberry juice
1 oz. lemon-lime soda
Dash lemon juice or squeeze fresh lemon

Shake the first four ingredients with ice and
strain into a martini glass. Add the dash of
lemon juice or squeeze of a fresh lemon.

White Grape on the Beach

1 oz. Smirnoff white grape-flavored vodka
¼ oz. peach schnapps
¼ oz. triple sec
Splash cranberry juice
Splash sweet and sour mix (Dissolve 1 tsp. sugar in 3 oz. water. Add 2 oz. lemon juice.)
Maraschino cherry for garnish

Shake liquids with ice. Strain into a martini glass. Garnish with the cherry.

White Peach

1½ oz. Stolichnaya citros vodka
1½ oz. Hiram Walker white peach schnapps
1 oz. cranberry juice
1 oz. pineapple juice
1 oz. sweet and sour mix (Dissolve 1 tsp. sugar in 3 oz. water. Add 2 oz. lemon juice.)
1 oz. lemon-lime soda
1 scoop rainbow sherbet

Build the first six ingredients in a glass over ice. Top with the scoop of sherbet.

White Peach Blossom Martini

1 oz. Stolichnaya ohranj vodka
1 oz. Hiram Walker white peach schnapps
½ oz. pineapple juice
Orange slice for garnish

Shake liquids with ice. Strain into a martini glass. Garnish with the orange slice.

White Peach Cobbler

Cinnamon sugar to rim glass
2 oz. Stolichnaya ohranj vodka
2 oz. Hiram Walker white peach schnapps
Hiram Walker white crème de cacao
2 oz. half-and-half
1 oz. cola
Peach slice for garnish

Rim a martini glass with cinnamon sugar. Shake the next four ingredients vigorously with ice, and strain into the martini glass. Top with the cola, and garnish with the peach slice.

White Peach Lemon Drop

Lemon juice to rim glass
Sugar to rim glass
2 oz. Stolichnaya ohranj vodka
1 oz. Hiram Walker white peach schnapps
1 oz. fresh lemon juice
½ oz. simple syrup (Dissolve 1 part sugar in 1
    part boiling water. Let cool.)

Rim a rocks glass with lemon juice and sugar.
Shake liquids vigorously with ice. Strain into
the glass.

White Peach Margarita

Salt to rim glass
2 oz. José Cuervo Especial tequila
1½ oz. Hiram Walker white peach schnapps
6 oz. sweet and sour mix (Dissolve 1 tsp.
    sugar in 3 oz. water. Add 2 oz. lemon
    juice.)
Lime corkscrew for garnish

Rim a 14-oz. glass with salt. Shake liquids vigorously with ice. Strain into the glass over ice.
Garnish with the lime corkscrew.

White Peach Paloma

Salt to rim glass
2 oz. José Cuervo Especial tequila
1½ oz. Hiram Walker white peach schnapps
5 oz. sweet and sour mix (Dissolve 1 tsp.
    sugar in 3 oz. water. Add 2 oz. lemon
    juice.)
2 oz. ruby red grapefruit juice
Lime corkscrew for garnish

Rim a 14-oz. glass with salt. Shake liquids vigorously with ice. Strain into the glass over ice. Garnish with the lime corkscrew.

White Peach Sangría

4 oz. Pinot Grigio
1½ oz. Malibu mango rum
1½ oz. Hiram Walker white peach schnapps
Squeeze lemon juice
Squeeze lime juice
Squeeze orange juice
3 oz. lemon-lime soda

Build the first six ingredients in a 14-oz. glass over ice. Pour back and forth in a shaker two times to mix, and top with the lemon-lime soda.

Wild Cosmopolitan

3 oz. Alizé wild passion
2 oz. citrus vodka
1 oz. fresh lime juice
Splash cranberry juice

Shake well, and serve straight up in a martini glass.

Yankee Doodle

4 slices fresh peeled ginger
5 large green grapes
1 tsp. raw sugar
1½ oz. SKYY Infusions grape vodka
Soda to top
Raspberries for garnish
Blueberries for garnish

Muddle the grapes, ginger, and sugar in a pint glass. Add ice and the vodka. Shake vigorously, and strain into a cocktail glass over ice. Top with the soda, and garnish with the raspberries and blueberries.

Yellow Fever

2 oz. Smirnoff vodka
Lemonade to fill

Serve in a tall glass over ice.

Summer Punches and Pitchers

Beach Bowl

Makes thirty 6-oz. drinks.

1½ bottles (750-mL) Bacardi rum
2 cups unsweetened pineapple juice
1 cup fresh lemon juice
½ pineapple, peeled, cored, and cut into
    wedges, plus extra for garnish
¼ cup simple syrup (Dissolve 1 part sugar in
    1 part boiling water. Let cool.)
2 liters club soda, chilled
Sliced strawberries for garnish

Mix the first five ingredients, and chill for 2 hours. Pour over ice into a punch bowl. Add the club soda. Add the sliced strawberries and pineapple chunks.

Berry Passionate Sangría

Serves 10–20.

1 bottle Merlot
1 cup Stolichnaya razberi vodka
1 cup Hiram Walker blueberry passion
    schnapps
12 lemon squeezes
12 lime squeezes
12 orange squeezes
2½ cups lemon-lime soda

Combine in a punch bowl half filled with ice.

Blushing White Peach Sangría

Serves 10–20.

1 bottle white Zinfandel
1¼ cup Hiram Walker white peach schnapps
1¼ cup pineapple juice
2½ cups lemon-lime soda
10 fresh peach slices
20 pineapple chunks

Combine the ingredients in a punch bowl half
filled with ice.

Campari Cherry Infusion

Serves 10–20.

2 liters Campari
4 liters SKYY Infusions citrus vodka
3 lb. cherries, stemmed and lightly macerated
¾ lb. dried apricots, sliced

Combine in a punch bowl half filled with ice.

Campari Citrus Infusion

Serves 10–20.

1 liter Campari
1 liter SKYY Infusions citrus vodka
1 gal. orange or tangerine juice
4 lemons, sliced
4 limes, sliced
4 oranges, sliced

Combine the ingredients in a punch bowl half filled with ice.

Champagne Sorbet Punch

Makes about 22 servings.

2 bottles Korbel brut champagne
1 bottle white wine
1 qt. lemon sherbet
Frozen lemon slices for garnish

Combine the first two ingredients in a punch bowl. Add lots of ice, then scoops of lemon sherbet. Garnish with the frozen lemon slices.

Confetti Punch

Makes twenty 6-oz. drinks.

6-oz. can frozen lemonade concentrate
6-oz. can frozen grapefruit concentrate
16-oz. can fruit cocktail
1 (750-mL.) bottle Bacardi superior rum
2 liters club soda, chilled

Mix the first four ingredients in a large container, and chill for 2 hours, stirring occasionally. To serve, pour into a punch bowl over ice. Add the club soda. Stir gently.

Cranberry Vodka Punch

Serves 10–20.

½ gal. Ocean Spray cranberry juice cocktail
1 bottle Wolfschmidt vodka
1 qt. ginger ale
1 qt. club soda
Pineapple chunks for garnish

Combine in a punch bowl half filled with ice.
Garnish with the pineapple chunks.

Deep Passion Punch

Serves 10–20.

2 cups Stolichnaya citros vodka
2 cups Malibu mango rum
2 cups Hiram Walker blueberry passion
    schnapps
5 cups sweet and sour mix (Dissolve 1 tsp.
    sugar in 3 oz. water. Add 2 oz. lemon
    juice.)
1½ cups ginger ale
1½ cups soda
1 qt. lemon or rainbow sherbet

Combine the first six ingredients in a punch
bowl half filled with ice. Scoop the sherbet into
balls, and float on top, or float the entire quart
of sherbet.

Fiery Fiesta Margarita

Serves 10–20.

1 (46-oz.) can Ocean Spray pineapple juice
1 mango, peeled, seeded, and sliced
2 cups José Cuervo golden margarita mix
3 large frozen strawberries
½ jalapeño pepper, seeded and cored, plus extra strips for garnish
4 tbsp. José Cuervo Especial tequila plus 1 tbsp. extra for garnish

Blend the first three ingredients with 3 cups ice until smooth. Add the frozen strawberries and jalapeño. Blend again until it looks like confetti. Place in a large, frozen margarita glass, and garnish with the tequila and jalapeño strips.

Fruit Punch à la Popov

Serves 10–20.

1½ cups finely diced fresh pineapple
1 bottle Popov vodka
1 cup Don Q Cristal rum
1 cup fresh lemon juice
1 cup orange juice
⅓ cup grenadine
1 qt. ginger ale, chilled
1 pt. strawberries, sliced

Combine the first five ingredients. Chill several hours or overnight. Place in a punch bowl. Add the grenadine, ginger ale, and strawberries. Add a block of ice, if desired.

Golden Spike Punch

Makes 16 drinks.

1 (46-oz.) can frozen grapefruit juice
1 (8-oz.) can apricot nectar
6 fresh mint leaves
½ cup sugar
2 cups Popov vodka
1 qt. club soda

Combine the first two ingredients, and mix well. Add some of the liquid to a few mint leaves in a cup, and muddle the leaves or crush them with a spoon. Add to the juice mixture. Add the sugar, and stir to dissolve. Pour over ice in a punch bowl, and add the vodka. Slowly pour the soda over the mixture, and stir gently.

Happy Hour Punch

Serves 10–20.

1 (750-mL) bottle Southern Comfort
1 cup pineapple juice
½ cup fresh lemon juice
1 cup grapefruit juice
2 qt. champagne or 7-Up
Orange slices decoratively cut for garnish

Chill liquids. Mix them in a punch bowl, adding champagne or 7-Up last. Add ice cubes, and garnish with the orange slices.

Lemon Champagne Punch

Makes about 11 cups.

Juice 6 lemons
1 cup sugar
1 bottle white wine
1 bottle pink champagne
1 bottle club soda
½ cup brandy
½ cup curaçao or other orange-flavored liqueur

In a punch bowl, combine lemon juice and sugar, and stir. Slowly add the wine, champagne, soda, brandy, and curaçao.

The Molly Pitcher

Serves 10–20.

1 bottle Laird's AppleJack
½ bottle Cointreau
5 oz. fresh lime juice
64 oz. cranberry juice
10 lime wheels for garnish

Mix over ice in a punch bowl. Garnish with the lime wheels.

One, Two Punch

Makes 18 servings.

46-oz. can fruit juicy red Hawaiian Punch
6-oz. can frozen orange juice

6-oz. can frozen lemonade
Block of ice
Mint leaves for garnish
Strawberry slices for garnish
Orange slices for garnish
Lemon slices for garnish
Lime slices for garnish
1 (750-mL) bottle Bacardi superior rum

Combine liquids, and chill for 2 hours. Pour punch over the block of ice in a punch bowl. Float the mint leaves, strawberries, orange, and lemon and lime slices on top. Serve in 6-oz. punch cups.

Open House Punch

Serves 10–20.

1 (750-mL) bottle Southern Comfort
6-oz. can frozen lemonade
6-oz. can frozen orange juice
3 qt. 7-Up
A few drops red food coloring
Block of ice
Orange slices for garnish
Lime slices for garnish

Chill ingredients. Mix in a punch bowl, adding the 7-Up last. Add the drops of red food coloring, as desired. Stir. Float a block of ice, and garnish with the orange and lime slices.

Patriotic Pleaser Cocktail (Red, White, and Booze)

Serves 10–20.

2 bottles José Cuervo margarita mix
3 scoops lemon sorbet
½ cup blue curaçao
½ cup whipped topping
4 strawberries for garnish

Blend the first two ingredients with 2 cups ice. In a small bowl, combine the whipped topping and blue curaçao. Pour the blended cocktail into a wine glass, and top with a layer of the blue topping. Garnish with a strawberry.

Rum-to-Tum

Makes 8 servings.

1½ cups Bacardi superior rum
2 cups pineapple juice
½ cup fresh lemon juice
¼ cup orange curaçao
¼ cup grenadine
1 liter chilled club soda
Half orange slices for garnish

Stir all ingredients in a 2½-qt. pitcher. Add ice cubes. Pour into 8-oz. glasses with ice. Garnish with the half orange slices.

Saronno Tee-Up

Serves 10–20.

1 qt. orange juice
¾ cup Disaronno amaretto
¾ cup gin
½ cup Ocean Spray pineapple juice
½ cup ginger ale
2 dashes Angostura bitters
Mint sprig for garnish

Place all ingredients in a 3-qt. pitcher half filled with ice cubes. Stir until cold. Serve in a tall glass with the mint sprig.

Saronno Top-Sider

Serves 10–20.

2 (12-oz.) cans apricot nectar, chilled
2 cups Disaronno amaretto
½ cup gin
Juice 1 large or 2 small limes
Lime slices for garnish

Pour into a 2½-qt. pitcher half filled with ice cubes. Stir until cold. Serve in tall glasses with ice garnished with the lime slices.

Sobieski "The Livin's Easy" Summer Punch

Serves 10–20.

1.75 liters Sobieski vodka
12¾ oz. Marie Brizard crème de cassis
16 oz. cold water
17 oz. orange juice
8½ oz. fresh lime juice
25½ oz. ginger ale, chilled
Lemon slices for garnish
Lime slices for garnish
Orange slices for garnish
Strawberry slices for garnish
Blueberries for garnish

Funnel all liquids except ginger ale into a large, sealable plastic container. Shake to incorporate all ingredients. Refrigerate for 30 minutes. Pour the mixture into a large decorative bowl over ice. Top with the chilled ginger ale, and stir gently. Garnish with the sliced lemons, limes, oranges, and thinly sliced ripe strawberries. Add a blueberry or two for anti-oxidation purposes. Serve and enjoy!

Tropical Punch

Serves 20.

1 (12-oz.) can fruit juicy red Hawaiian Punch
1 (12-oz.) can orange juice concentrate
1 (12-oz.) can lemonade or limeade concentrate
1 liter light rum
Strawberries for garnish
Orange slices for garnish
Lemon slices for garnish
Lime slices for garnish

Mix liquids in a large container. Chill for 2 hours. Pour the mixture over ice in a punch bowl. Float the strawberries and slices of oranges, lemons, and limes.

White Peach Punch

Serves 10–20.

2 cups Stolichnaya citros vodka
2 cups Hiram Walker white peach schnapps
1¼ cups cranberry juice
1¼ cups pineapple juice
2½ cups sweet and sour mix (Dissolve 1 tsp. sugar in 3 oz. water. Add 2 oz. lemon juice.)
2½ cups lemon-lime soda
1 scoop rainbow sherbet

Combine liquids in a punch bowl quarter filled with ice. Scoop the sherbet into balls, and float on top, or float the entire quart of sherbet.

White Sangría

Serves 10–20.

2 cups Livingston Chablis Blanc
1 oz. cherry brandy
16 oz. club soda
Thinly sliced fresh citrus fruit of your choice
Red Maraschino cherries with stems
Thinly sliced fresh lime for garnish

Combine the first five ingredients in a punch bowl over a generous amount of ice, and garnish with the lime slices.

SUMMER RECIPES

Bacardi Lime Sherbet

Makes 4–6 servings.

1 cup fresh lime juice
4 tsp. Sweet 'N Low or other sugar substitute
Rinds 12 limes, grated
1½ tbsp. Bacardi superior rum
Mint sprigs for garnish

Combine 2 cups water and the lime juice in a
2-qt. saucepan. Dissolve the sugar substitute in
this mixture. Heat the saucepan over low heat,
and slowly bring to a boil. When the mixture
boils, cook for exactly 5 minutes. Remove from
the heat, and cool to room temperature. Add
the grated rinds. Transfer the mixture to an
ice tray or shallow bowl. Freeze for at least 5
hours, scraping the sides of the pan into the
mixture every hour. Spoon the sherbet into
dessert glasses. Splash the tops of each serving with 1 tsp. rum, and garnish with a sprig
of mint.

Brown Ale Crêpes with Cranberry-Orange Lager Sauce

Serves 4.

For Cranberry-Orange Lager Sauce
2 cups orange juice
1 cup lager
1 cup sugar
2 tbsp. cornstarch
1 (12-oz.) bag cranberries

For Brown Ale Crêpes
1 (12-oz.) bottle brown ale
¾ cup milk
3 large eggs
3 tbsp. sugar
3 tbsp. melted butter
2 cups all-purpose flour
½ tsp. salt

For Ricotta Cheese Filling
1 (3-lb.) container whole-milk ricotta cheese
3 tbsp. honey
1½ tsp. grated lemon zest
2 tbsp. fresh lemon juice
½ tsp. ground cinnamon

To Make Cranberry-Orange Lager Sauce
Whisk together the orange juice, lager, sugar, and cornstarch until blended in a large sauce-pan. Add the cranberries. Over medium-high heat, bring the mixture to a boil. Reduce the heat to medium-low, and cook for 15 minutes, or until the sauce thickens slightly and the cranberries pop. If serving immediately, keep

the sauce warm; or cool, cover, and refrigerate for up to 4 days.

To Make Brown Ale Crêpes
Whisk together the ale, milk, eggs, sugar, and butter in a large bowl until well blended. Whisk in the flour and salt until the batter is very smooth, for 2 to 3 minutes. Let the batter rest for 20 minutes.

Preheat an 8- or 9-inch nonstick crêpe pan or skillet over medium heat. When the pan is hot, remove from the heat, and spray with cooking spray. Add ¼-cup batter to the pan. Tilt the pan to spread the batter into a 7-inch round. Return the pan to the heat, and lightly brown the crêpe about 45 seconds, or until the edges start to curl. Turn the crêpe over, and cook the second side 30 to 45 seconds longer, or until lightly browned. Transfer to a plate. Repeat with the remaining batter to make 20 crêpes. These may be made several days ahead, stacked between layers of waxed or parchment paper, covered, and refrigerated.

To Make Ricotta Cheese Filling
In a large bowl combine ricotta cheese, honey, lemon zest, lemon juice, and cinnamon. Stir well to blend. The filling may be made several days ahead, covered, and refrigerated.

To Assemble Crêpes
Preheat the oven to 350 degrees. Lightly coat 2 shallow baking pans or dishes with nonstick spray. For each crêpe, place 2 rounded tbsp. filling in the center in a 3-inch-long mound. Fold two opposite edges of the crêpe over the filling; fold in remaining edges to form a

packet. Place crêpes in the prepared baking dish. Repeat with the remaining filling and crêpes. Bake 15 minutes, or until heated throughout and slightly crisp. Top with Cranberry-Orange Lager Sauce.

Burgers With Bacardi Onions

Makes 2 cups.

2 tbsp. butter or margarine
3 cups sliced onion
½ cup 80-proof Bacardi superior or Bacardi gold rum
1 tsp. sugar
¼ tsp. salt
Freshly ground pepper to taste

Melt the butter in a heavy skillet over low or medium heat. Add the onions, and sauté about 10 minutes or until lightly browned. Add the rum, sugar, salt, and pepper. Cook, stirring until the liquid evaporates. Serve over hamburgers.

Canadian Club Blue Cheese Ball

Makes 10–12 servings.

2 (8-oz.) packages cream cheese, softened
¾ cups crumbled blue cheese, softened
1 cup shredded cheddar cheese
2–3 tbsp. grated onion
2 tbsp. Canadian Club
½ cup toasted slivered almonds

Beat together the cream cheese and blue cheese. Stir in the cheddar cheese, onion, and Canadian Club. Shape into a ball, roll in slivered almonds, and refrigerate until firm, about 2 hours. Serve with crackers.

Chipotle Shrimp and Lager Beer Salad

Makes 6 servings.

24 large shrimp (about 1 lb.), peeled, with
　　shells intact
1 (12-oz.) bottle lager or golden ale
3 cloves garlic, smashed
¼ tsp. salt
3 chipotle peppers in adobo sauce, minced
2 tsp. adobo sauce
⅔ cup mayonnaise
¼ cup chili sauce
1 tbsp. fresh lime juice
1 tbsp. fresh chives, chopped
3 cups arugula or other lettuce leaves
1 avocado, peeled and diced
½ pt. grape tomatoes
Tortilla chips

Lay the shrimp in a single layer in a large skillet. Add the beer, garlic, and salt. Turn heat to medium-low, and slowly poach the shrimp, turning often, until cooked through, for 6 to 8 minutes. Using a slotted spoon, remove the shrimp to a bowl. Chill.

Boil the poaching liquid about 6 minutes, or until reduced to ¼ cup. Pour the liquid into a small bowl; mash garlic into beer reduction with a fork. Cool. Stir in peppers, adobo sauce, mayonnaise, chili sauce, lime juice, and chives. Chill.

To serve, line plates with the arugula or lettuce leaves. Top with the shrimp, avocado, and tomatoes. Serve with the chipotle cocktail sauce and tortilla chips.

Chuckwagon Pot Roast

Makes 6 to 8 servings.

2 slices bacon
1 carrot, peeled and diced
1 onion, diced
3–4 lb. beef chuck roast
3 tbsp. all-purpose flour
3 tbsp. tomato paste
2 tbsp. tequila
2 cubes beef bouillon
2 cups red table wine
1 tbsp. Tabasco
2 bay leaves
1 tbsp. salt

Cook bacon until crisp in a Dutch oven over medium heat; remove to paper towels. Add the carrot and onion, and cook 2 minutes. Remove the vegetables, and set aside. Crumble the bacon, and set aside.

Dredge the roast with flour, and place in hot drippings; cook, turning, until brown on all sides. Add the vegetables, bacon, and remaining ingredients, and mix well. Bring to a boil; reduce heat to medium-low, cover, and cook 2 hours, or until meat is tender. When the meat is done, remove from the pan, and cut into slices; pour the sauce over the meat.

Coco Chocolate Mousse

Makes 16 (½-cup) servings.

1½ cups Coco Lopez cream of coconut
⅔ cup instant chocolate-pudding mix
⅔ cup cocoa
3 cups heavy cream, whipped

Combine cream of coconut, pudding mix, ½ cup water, and cocoa in a mixer bowl. On low speed, beat mixture until smooth and creamy, about 2 minutes. Do not overmix. Fold in the whipped cream. Spoon ½ cup of the mixture into individual dishes. Chill. Refrigerate unused servings.

Coconut Chicken Fingers

Makes 16 (4-oz.) servings.

4 lb. boneless, skinless chicken breast halves
   or chicken breast tenderloins
3 cups Coco Lopez cream of coconut
1 qt. pineapple juice
2 tsp. salt
1 tbsp. white pepper
3 cups flat beer
6 whole eggs
3 cups all-purpose flour, unsifted
¼ cup paprika
1 tbsp. salt
1 tbsp. white pepper
2 cups flaked coconut, optional
Vegetable oil

Cut the chicken into 1x3-inch strips. In a bowl,
combine the cream of coconut, pineapple
juice, salt, and pepper. Pour over the chicken.
Cover, and refrigerate overnight. In a mixing
bowl, beat together the beer and eggs. On
low speed, gradually add flour, paprika, salt,
and pepper; mix until smooth. Dip chicken
strips into batter and flaked coconut. Heat the
vegetable oil to 325 degrees in a deep fryer
or pot. Fry the strips in oil until golden brown.
Serve hot.

Empanadas

Makes 10 servings.

1 large pkg. store-bought empanada dough
 (freezer section)
1 tbsp. olive oil
1 large onion
1 lb. ground turkey
1 large pkg. taco seasoning
½ cup José Cuervo golden margarita mix
Canola oil for frying
Sour cream
Salsa

Heat the oil on medium to high heat in a large skillet. Add the onion, and sauté until golden. Add the ground turkey, and cook until well done. Mix in the taco seasoning packet and margarita mix, and cook until all of the liquid is absorbed.

Heat another large skillet with ¼ inch canola oil to 350 degrees. Place 2 tbsp. mix in the center of one of the dough rounds. Fold it over to form a half circle. Press down on the open edges with a fork to seal. Repeat with the remaining dough rounds.

Add the empanadas to the oil, and fry in batches until golden. Remove and drain on paper-towel-lined plate. Serve with sour cream and salsa.

Fried Plantains with Cuervo Cream Sauce

Makes 4 servings.

1–3 tbsp. peanut oil
4 green plantains, peeled and sliced on bias
   into 2-inch pieces
Kosher salt to taste
1 bottle José Cuervo margarita mix
3 tbsp. butter
1 tsp. flour
½ cup confectioners' sugar
¼ cup heavy cream

To Make Plantains
Heat the oil in a cast-iron skillet to 365 degrees. Smash the plantains to flatten.

Fry the plantains in batches until golden brown. Using a slotted spoon, remove them to a plate lined with paper towels, and season with salt to taste.

To Make Cuervo Cream Sauce
Melt the butter in a second skillet over medium heat, and add the flour. Sauté for 2 minutes to make a roux.

Add the margarita mix, and cook until reduced by half. Add the sugar and cream, and cook for 2 minutes more. Pour over the plantains, and serve.

Golden Goodness Bars

Makes 16 bars.

For the Base
1 cup all-purpose flour
¾ cup sugar
½ tsp. baking powder
2 cups puffed square rice cereal
¼ lb. (1 stick) butter, cut into pieces

For the Topping
3 eggs, beaten
3 tbsp. all-purpose flour
½ tsp. baking powder
Zest of 1 orange
⅓ cup José Cuervo golden margarita mix
Confectioners' sugar for sprinkling

Preheat the oven to 350 degrees. Butter a 9 x 9-inch-square baking pan.

Place the flour, sugar, baking powder, and cereal in a food processor, and pulse to combine into coarse crumbs. Add the butter, a little at a time, and pulse again until it forms wet, coarse crumbs. Make sure not to overprocess. Press the crumb mixture evenly and firmly on the bottom of the buttered pan.

Bake for 12–15 minutes, or until golden.

In a medium bowl whisk all the ingredients for the topping together. Pour them into the hot crust. Return the pan to the oven, and bake for another 12–15 minutes more. The top should be set, but not browned. Let cool, cut into bars, and sprinkle with confectioners' sugar.

Green Olive-Chili Beer Dip

Makes 8 (1¾ cup) servings.

1 Serrano chile
1 (12-oz.) bottle pale lager
3 tbsp. extra virgin olive oil
1 onion, chopped
4 cloves garlic, coarsely chopped
1 (16-oz.) jar large pitted, stuffed green
  olives, drained
¼ cup tahini (sesame seed paste)
1½ tbsp. lemon juice
1 tsp. honey
½ tsp. ground coriander
¼ tsp. ground cumin
¼ tsp. black pepper
¼ cup finely chopped cilantro
1 plum tomato, diced
2 tbsp. coarsely chopped unsalted pistachios
½ tsp. kosher salt
Toasted bread, warm sliced pita, or pita chips

Make slit in one side of the chile; place it in a small saucepan over medium heat. Add the beer; bring to boil. Remove from the heat, and cover. Let steep 1 hour to make Chili Beer.

Heat 2 tbsp. of the oil in a large skillet over medium heat; add the onion and garlic. Sauté 3 minutes; add the olives, and sauté 2 minutes more. Add the Chili Beer and chile; boil 10 minutes, or until most of the beer has cooked away. Cool to room temperature.

Transfer olive mixture to a food processor; add the tahini, lemon juice, honey, coriander, cumin, and pepper. Process until smooth, with some pieces of olive still visible. Stir in cilantro. Spread mixture on a plate or in a shallow soup bowl; cover and refrigerate 1 hour to allow flavors to blend.

To serve, place on platter, scatter the top of the dip with tomatoes and pistachios, sprinkle with salt, and drizzle the remaining 1 tbsp. olive oil over the top. Serve with toasted bread, warm sliced pita, or pita chips.

Grilled Honey-Bourbon Turkey

Makes 4 servings.

1 (6-lb.) whole turkey breast

For Marinade
1 cup Evan Williams bourbon
½ cup dry sherry
⅓ cup soy sauce
¼ cup dry red wine
3 tbsp. vegetable oil
2 tbsp. sugar
2 tbsp. chopped fresh rosemary
Freshly ground black pepper, to taste

For Glaze
¾ cup Evan Williams bourbon
⅓ cup honey
⅓ cup ketchup
2 tbsp. firmly packed brown sugar

Place turkey in a large bowl or 1-gal. ziplock bag. Stir together marinade ingredients, and pour over turkey. Marinate at least 2 hours, preferably overnight in a refrigerator.

Remove the turkey from the marinade, and grill, about 12 minutes per pound. Stir together the glaze ingredients in a bowl. Brush the glaze onto the turkey after about 40 minutes on the grill, and again when the turkey is removed. Slice, and serve on a platter.

Harvey Wallbanger Cake

Makes 6 servings.

1 box Duncan Hines yellow cake mix
1 (¾-oz.) package vanilla instant pudding
½ cup vegetable oil
4 large eggs
¼ cup vodka
¼ cup Galliano
⅔ cup orange juice
Confectioners' sugar for dusting

Preheat the oven to 350 degrees. Grease a Bundt pan. Combine all the ingredients in a large bowl, and beat until well mixed. Pour into the Bundt pan.

Bake for 45–50 minutes. (If using convection oven, bake at 335 degrees for about 35–40 minutes.) Cool and dust with confectioners' sugar.

From Dianne Cifelli

Hot Dogs and Bacardi Relish

Makes 2 cups.

2 cloves garlic
½ small onion, cut into large pieces
1 red pepper, chopped
8-oz. jar sweet gherkins, drained
¼ cup Bacardi rum

In a food processor or blender, process the garlic until very finely chopped. Add the onion, red pepper, gherkins, and rum. Pulse until finely chopped.

Italian Meatball, Pasta, and Wheat Beer Soup

Makes 6 servings.

2 (14.5-oz.) cans reduced-sodium beef broth
1 (14.5-oz.) can chicken broth
1 (14.5-oz.) can diced tomatoes, Italian herb
    flavor, undrained
1 (12-oz.) bottle wheat beer
1 bunch escarole, core removed, cut cross-
    wise into 1-inch pieces
2 cups shredded or chopped carrots
½ cup chopped onion
¼ cup shredded Parmesan cheese
1 (1-lb.) package frozen Italian meatballs
1 cup dried small pasta, such as fiori, small
    penne, or small shell

In a soup pot, combine beef broth, chicken broth, tomatoes and juices, wheat beer, escarole leaves, carrots, onion, Parmesan cheese, and meatballs. Bring to a boil; reduce the heat to low, cover the pot, and cook for 30 minutes.

Stir in the pasta. Increase the heat to medium-low, cover, and cook 11 minutes, or until pasta is just tender. Remove the soup from heat; let stand 5 minutes before serving.

Jerked Chicken

2 tsp. ground cinnamon
2 tsp. ground allspice
1 tsp. ground nutmeg
2 tsp. ground black pepper
8 scallions, minced
½ cup Meyer's rum
2 tbsp. vegetable oil
2 (4-lb.) chickens, quartered

Preheat the oven to 300 degrees.

Combine the seasonings and scallions; add the oil, and stir into the rum. Pour over the chicken.

Bake, basting frequently, for 1¼ hours, or until juices run clear.

Kicked-Up Cuervo Ribs

Makes 6 servings.

2 tbsp. olive oil
½ cup finely chopped Vidalia onions
4 garlic cloves, smashed
1 jalapeño pepper, finely chopped
1 (15.5-oz) jar commercial salsa, pureed
    (mild, medium, or hot)
Juice 1 lime
1 tbsp. Dijon mustard
1 tbsp. Worcestershire sauce
2 tbsp. honey
1 bottle José Cuervo margarita mix
2 racks baby back ribs
Olive oil
Salt and freshly ground black pepper to taste
Smoked paprika

Preheat the grill or oven to 400 degrees.

Heat the oil in a heavy skillet over medium heat, and add the onions, garlic, and jalapeño, then sauté until soft. Add the next six ingredients, and bring to a boil. Reduce the heat to low, and cook for 35–45 minutes.

Rub the ribs with olive oil, and season with salt, pepper, and paprika. Place them in the center of a large piece of aluminum foil, and wrap them up. Make sure to secure the sides well but keep the foil around the ribs loose.

Roast the ribs in the foil either on the grill or in the oven for 30–40 minutes.

Carefully remove the ribs from the foil, and baste them with the sauce. Grill or broil the ribs for about 4 minutes per side, basting to encrust flavor. Slice and serve.

Margarita Fruit Salad

Makes 8 servings.

For Tequila-Orange Liqueur Dressing
½ cup José Cuervo golden margarita mix
3 tbsp. orange marmalade
Juice of 1 lime, about 2 tbsp.

For Fruit Salad
4 cups fresh sliced strawberries
4 oranges, peeled and sectioned
1 small honeydew melon, rind and seeds
    removed, cubed
1 small cantaloupe, rind and seeds removed,
    cubed
1 small pineapple, peeled and rind removed,
    cubed
½ cup thinly sliced fresh mint leaves

In a large bowl, mix together the margarita mix, orange marmalade, and lime juice. Add the fruit, and stir to combine. Refrigerate for several hours or overnight to allow the flavors to blend. Add mint, toss, and serve.

Maria's Fajitas

Makes 6 servings.

For Marinated Beef
¼ cup silver tequila
1 tbsp. lime juice
1 tbsp. soy sauce
1½ tsp. Tabasco
¼ tsp. ground black pepper
2½ lb. (½-inch-thick) beef top sirloin,
    trimmed

For Pico de Gallo
¼ cup chopped fresh New Mexican green
    chiles
¼ cup chopped jalapeño chiles
¼ cup chopped tomatoes
¼ cup chopped onions
1½ tsp. Tabasco
1 clove garlic, minced

For Fajitas
2 tbsp. vegetable oil
2 green bell peppers, cut into strips
2 medium onions, halved and sliced
2 medium tomatoes, diced
Flour tortillas
Guacamole
Sour cream

To Make Marinated Beef
Combine the tequila, lime juice, soy sauce,
Tabasco, and black pepper in a large bowl;
mix well. Drain steaks, and grill over medium-
high heat to desired doneness. Let stand 5
minutes; cut into 3 x ¼-inch strips. Add beef,

and toss to coat well; cover, and refrigerate for 24 hours, turning meat occasionally.

To Make Pico de Gallo
Combine all pico de gallo ingredients in a small bowl, and mix well; cover and chill for 1 hour.

To Make Fajitas
Heat the oil in a large skillet over high heat. Add peppers, onions, and tomatoes, and sauté until softened, about 5 minutes. Add beef and cook 5 minutes more. If desired, pour mixture into a preheated cast-iron fajita pan and serve sizzling.

To serve, spoon meat mixture onto flour tortillas; top with pico de gallo, guacamole, and sour cream.

Peachtree Tropical Salad

Serves 4–6.

1½ cups peeled, sliced fresh ripe peaches
¼ cup sugar
1 can pineapple chunks
1 cup flaked coconut
1 cup chopped walnuts
1 cup sour cream
½ cup DeKuyper peachtree schnapps
1 cup small marshmallows

Combine the peaches and sugar, and mix gently so as not to break slices. Cover, and refrigerate for 1 to 2 hours. After peaches have chilled, place them in a large bowl, and add the pineapple, coconut, and walnuts. Mix sour cream and schnapps together, and pour over the ingredients. Toss gently, cover, and refrigerate for 4 to 8 hours. Garnish with the marshmallows before serving.

Potted Bock Beer and Brie Spread

Makes 8 servings.

2 wheels baby Brie (about 13 oz. each), rinds
  removed
4 oz. sharp white cheddar cheese, cut into
  chunks
²⁄₃ cup pale bock beer
¹⁄₃ cup finely diced sun-dried tomatoes
1 tbsp. horseradish sauce
1 tbsp. white wine Worcestershire sauce
½ tsp. freshly ground black pepper
¼ cup chopped parsley
Crackers, raw vegetables, and/or breadsticks
  for serving

Cut the Brie cheese into small chunks; place in
food processor with cheddar cheese chunks,
beer, sun-dried tomatoes, horseradish sauce,
Worcestershire sauce, and pepper. Pulse mixture, scraping down the sides of the bowl with
a rubber spatula, until mixture is fairly smooth,
but with some bits of cheese still present.

Add parsley. Pulse mixture just to incorporate.
If mixture remains too thick, work in a little
more beer until desired spreading consistency
is reached. Pack into two (2-cup) crocks; cover
the surface with plastic wrap. Refrigerate at
least 1 day before serving to allow flavors to
blend. (Spread may be made up to 1 week
ahead and refrigerated.) Let spread come to
room temperature before serving.

Tecate Light Sauce

Serves 4–6.

1 can Tecate Light beer
1 oz. olive oil
1 tsp. salt
1 tsp. black pepper
1 tsp. minced garlic
1 tsp. minced onion
2 lb. chicken or beef

Mix ingredients in a large bowl. Cover chicken or beef with marinade, and allow to rest for 3–4 hours. Cook over hot grill until well done.

Tequila-Marinated London Broil

1 jalapeño chile, seeded
1 clove garlic
1 cup tequila
1 cup teriyaki sauce
¼ cup sesame oil
¼ cup Worcestershire sauce
¼ teaspoon kosher salt
¼ teaspoon fresh ground black pepper
3½ lb. London broil

Blend all the ingredients except the meat until smooth. Place the meat in a dish or plastic bag, pour the marinade over the meat, and turn to coat. Refrigerate for at least 4 to 6 hours before cooking.

Preheat grill to high; grill meat until done to your preference. Enjoy!

VO Shish Kebab

Makes 6 servings.

2 lb. boneless lean lamb, cut into 2-inch cubes
1 cup Seagram's VO whiskey
3 tbsp. Worcestershire sauce
2 tsp. garlic salt
½ tsp. pepper
3 large basil leaves, finely chopped
1 large green pepper
1 large onion
1 pt. cherry tomatoes

In a bowl, mix the whiskey, Worcestershire sauce, garlic salt, pepper, and basil in a bowl. Put the lamb into the bowl, and stir. Marinate at room temperature for 2 hours; stir often.

Preheat the broiler.

Cut the pepper and onion into 1-inch pieces. Drain the excess marinade off the lamb and set the marinade aside. On each of 8 metal skewers, alternate tomatoes and pieces of meat, pepper, and onion, leaving a small space between each. Place on the broiler pan rack. Broil for about 20 minutes, turning and brushing often with marinade to brown evenly. Remove from the oven, and brush lightly with extra marinade. Serve at once.

Glossary

Tools You Will Need

Bar Spoon: A long spoon for stirring cocktails or liquids in pitchers.

Blender: For blending drinks or crushing ice. Remember to save your blade by always pouring in the liquid before the ice.

Cocktail Shaker and Mixing/Measuring Glass: There are countless designs to choose from, but the standard is the Boston. It's a mixing glass that fits snugly into a stainless steel cone.

Ice Bag: To crush ice, use a rubber mallet and a lint-free or canvas ice bag, often referred to as a Lewis ice bag.

Ice Bucket: This should have a vacuum seal and the capacity to hold three trays of ice.

Ice Scoop/Tongs/Ice Pick: Never use your hands to pick up ice; use a scoop or tongs. The ice pick can help you unstick ice or break it up.

Jigger/Measuring Glass: Glass or metal, all drinks should be made using these bar tools. Remember that drinks on the rocks and mixed drinks should contain no more than 2 oz. alcohol.

Knife and Cutting Board: A sturdy board and a small, very sharp paring knife are essential to cutting fruit garnishes.

Muddler: Use this small wooden bat or pestle to crush fruit, herbs, or cracked ice. Muddlers come in all different sizes and are used for making stixx drinks.

Napkins/Coasters: To place a drink on, hold a drink with, and for basic convenience.

Pitcher of Water: Keep it clean. Someone always wants water, and you certainly will use it.

Pourer: This provides a helpful way to pour directly into the glass. A lidded spout helps keep everything but the drink out.

Stirrers/Straws: Use them to sip, stir, and mix drinks. Glass is preferred for the mixer/stirrer. They can be custom molded and come in all different shapes and colors. (www.bradnedstirs.com/printabledrinkstirs.html)

Strainer: The strainer, quite simply, prevents ice from pouring out of the shaker. The two most common types in use are the Hawthorne and the Julep. The Hawthorne, with its distinctive coil rim, is most often used when pouring from the metal part of the Boston shaker. The Julep is a perforated metal spoon-like strainer used when pouring from the glass part of the Boston.

Swizzle Stick: A fancy stirrer, oftentimes with the establishment's name on it.

Wine/Bottle Opener: They come in all shapes and sizes; the best is the industry-standard waiter's opener. It opens cans as well as snaps off those bottle tops, and it has a sharp blade.

GLASSWARE

Brandy Snifters: Smaller sizes of the glasses, which range in size from 5½ to 22 oz., are perfect for serving cognac, liqueur, and premium whiskey. The larger sizes provide enough space for a noseful of aroma, and the small stems on large bowls allow a cupped hand to warm the liquid.

Champagne Glass: A narrow version of the standard wine glass has a tapered bowl to prevent those tiny bubbles from escaping and is usually never more than half filled. Also preferable for any sparkling liquid, including ciders.

Cocktail or Martini Glass: These glasses are perfect for martinis and Manhattans. Remember that the stem is not just for show; it keeps hands from warming the drink. Available in 3- to 6-oz. sizes.

Coolers: These large-capacity tumblers are taller and hold a lot of ice for larger concoctions. They have become popular as of late for non-alcoholic and extra-volume highballs.

Highball Glass: Extremely versatile glass available in many sizes and used for almost any drink. Usually clear and tall, the most popular sizes range from 8 to 12 oz.

Hurricane Glass: Tropical fruit drinks and bloody Marys are perfectly suited for these 16- to 23-oz. tall, curved glasses.

Rocks Glasses: These "old-fashioned" glasses hold from 6 to 10 oz. and are used for on-the-rocks presentations. Double rocks will run between 12 and 15 oz.

Shot Glass: The old standby can also be used as a measuring glass and is a must for every bar.

Mixing Terms

Build: In a glass full of ice, first pour in the liquor or spirit, then add the mixer. Add stirring/swizzle stick to stir the cocktail.

Fill: After you add ice and liquor or spirits, fill with mixer to within one-quarter inch of the top.

Floating: To layer one ingredient on the top of a shot or cocktail.

Layering: Topping one ingredient over another.

Types of Drinks

Apéritif: A light alcohol drink served before lunch or dinner, sometimes bitter.

Blended Drinks: Blender drinks consisting of ice, ice cream, and a variety of other ingredients blended until smooth though thick in consistency.

Cobbler: A tall drink usually filled with crushed ice and garnished with fruit or mint.

Cream: Any drink made with ice cream, heavy cream, half-and-half, or any of the famous bottled cream drinks.

Crusta: Served in a wine glass with sugar-coated rim and the inside of the glass lined with a citrus rind.

Cups: A traditionally British category of wine-based drinks.

Daisy: An oversized cocktail sweetened with fruit syrup served over crushed ice.

Eggnog: A blend of milk or cream, beaten eggs, sugar, and liquor, usually rum, brandy, or whiskey and sometimes sherry, topped with nutmeg.

Flip: Cold, creamy drinks made with eggs, sugar, alcohol, and citrus juice.

Highball: A tall drink usually served with whiskey and ginger ale. The favorite drink of many drinkers' grandparents.

Grog: A rum-based drink made with fruit and sugar.

Julep: A tall, sweet drink usually made with bourbon, water, sugar, crushed ice, and occasionally mint. The most popular julep is, of course, the Kentucky Derby's famous Mint Julep.

Mist: Any type of alcoholic beverage served over crushed ice.

Mojito: A Cuban-born drink prepared with sugar, muddled mint leaves, fresh lime juice, rum, ice, soda water, and garnished with mint leaves.

Puff: Made with equal parts alcohol and milk, topped with club soda.

Pousse-Café: A drink made with layers created by floating liqueurs according to their density.

Rickey: A cocktail made of alcohol (usually whiskey, lime juice, and soda water).

Shooter: A straight shot of alcohol, also sometimes called serving a drink "neat."

Sling: A tall drink made with lemon juice and sugar, topped with club soda.

Sours: Drinks made with lemon juice, sugar, and alcohol.

Stixx: Tall, muddled cocktails using different sized muddlers from 6 inches to 12 inches.

Now they are muddling herbs, fruits, spices, and a variety of ethnic and regional ingredients including beans, roots, and spices.

Toddy: Served hot, it's a mixture of alcohol, spices, and hot water.

Toppers: Blended drinks with ice cream or crushed ice, the thicker the better, which is why these drinks are served with a spoon and a straw. They are made using cordials, flavored rums, flavored vodkas, blended fresh fruits, and tropical juices. They are topped with crushed candy, fruits, nuts, and just about anything you can eat with a spoon.

How to Rim Your Glass

Coating the rim of a glass with salt, sugar, or any other like substance adds a decorative touch that improves the presentation of the cocktail.

Simple steps:

1. Moisten the rim of the glass (a lime wedge to rim a margarita; water or liqueur to sugar-rim for Kahlúa or a chocolate martini).

2. Dip the rim in whatever ingredient you want to coat the glass with.

3. Slowly turn the glass to ensure you coat evenly.

4. Shake off any excess.

5. Fill the glass with your prepared cocktail.

For more information and different cocktail rimmers, go to www.stirrings.com.

Index

C

D

E

F

G

About the Author

Ray Foley, a former Marine with over thirty years of bartending and restaurant experience, is the founder and publisher of *Bartender Magazine,* the only magazine in the world specifically geared toward bartenders and one of the very few primarily designed for servers of alcohol. *Bartender Magazine* is enjoying its twenty-ninth year. It currently has a circulation of over 148,000, and the circulation is steadily growing.

Mr. Foley serves as a consultant to some of our nation's foremost distillers and importers. He is also responsible for naming and inventing new drinks for the liquor industry, including "The Fuzzy Navel," "The Royal Stretch," "S.O.B," and "The Royal Turf."

He is also the author of: *The Ultimate Cocktail Book; The Ultimate Little Shooter Book; The Ultimate Little Martini Book; The Ultimate Little Frozen Drink Book; Advice from Anonymous; Spirits of Ireland; Beer Is the Answer, I Forgot the Question; X-Rated Drink Book; Bartending for Dummies; How to Run a Bar for Dummies; Bartender Magazine's Ultimate Bartender's Guide; The Vodka 1000; The Tequila 1000;* and *The Rum 1000.*

Ray resides in New Jersey with his wife and partner of twenty-five years, Jackie, and their son, Ryan. He is also the father of three other wonderful and bright children: Raymond Pindar, William, and Amy.

Mr. Foley is foremost and always will be a bartender.

For more information, please contact Jackie Foley at *Bartender Magazine,* P.O. Box 158, Liberty Corner, NJ, 07938. Telephone: (908) 766-6006; fax: (908) 766-6607; email: barmag@aol.com; website: www.bartender.com.